STAR WARS

THE OFFICIAL CROCHET PATTERN BOOK

STAR WARS

THE OFFICIAL CROCHET PATTERN BOOK

CROCHET YOUR WAY THROUGH THE GALAXY

LEAH PARKER

CONTENTS

7 Introduction

SECTION 1: TOYS & AMIGURUMI

11 Lightsabers
17 Ewok Amigurumi
23 Jawa Amigurumi
27 Mace Windu Amigurumi
33 Lando Calrissian Amigurumi
39 Darth Maul Amigurumi
45 Stormtrooper Doll

SECTION 2: COSTUMES

51 Ahsoka Tano's Ruana Wrap
55 Han Solo's Vest
63 Phantom Menace Scarf
67 Jyn Erso's Hooded Cowl
71 Padmé Amidala's Battle Wrap

SECTION 3: INSPIRED CLOTHING

77 Aki-Aki Festival of the Ancestors Shawl
81 Tauntaun Cowl
85 Ewok Toque
89 Handmaiden-Inspired Jumper
93 Long Hooded Scarf
97 Grogu Bonnet
101 Chewbacca Bandolier Scarf

SECTION 4: HOME DÉCOR & GIFTS

109 "It's a Trap" Bath Mat
117 BB-8 Tea Cosy
121 Imperial Trivet
125 Tatooine Landscape Blanket
135 Yoda Coaster

139 Abbreviations
139 Yarn Resource Guide
140 Acknowledgements
143 About the Author

SKILL LEVELS

/ BEGINNER
// ADVANCED BEGINNER
/// INTERMEDIATE
//// ADVANCED

Audiences were first introduced to George Lucas's vast *Star Wars* galaxy in 1977, with the premiere of *Star Wars*: Episode IV—*A New Hope*. That film became an instant classic, as well as the start of an epic landscape of interconnected stories that have expanded into multiple films, TV series, and books. Set "a long time ago in a galaxy far, far away," *Star Wars* chronicles the lives and quests of brave rebels as they take on corrupt Imperial forces with a powerful reach. It's a battle of good versus evil on a massive scale, fought with incredible technology, across unique planets with their own distinct environments, vivid cultures, and long-standing traditions. These are worlds populated with determined droids, princesses who do their own rescuing, and smugglers or bounty hunters occasionally willing to put their own interests aside for the greater good.

From Coruscant to the Outer Rim, this book offers crochet projects inspired by every corner of the *Star Wars* galaxy. Take a trip to the Aki-Aki Festival of the Ancestors with a brightly colored wrap, or visit Tatooine with a blanket inspired by the planet's iconic sunsets. Revisit some of your favourite characters, from Mace Windu to Darth Maul, while honing your amigurumi skills. You can even create your very own lightsaber or a homemade version of Han Solo's vest. Alongside these patterns, you'll find behind-the-scenes facts, iconic quotes, and a recounting of major moments from the films, all designed to take you deeper into the *Star Wars* galaxy.

On a personal note, I vividly remember sitting in the theater watching *Star Wars:* Episode III—*Revenge of the Sith*, thinking how lucky everyone involved in the films must have felt to be a part of something so special and beloved. I dreamed of finding my own small place in that galaxy, and I am beyond thrilled that this dream has become a reality with this book. My hope is that these patterns give you a chance to do the same and bring a little bit of *Star Wars* to your daily life. So, pick up your lightsabers (or, in this case, your crochet hooks) and begin your journey crocheting your way through the galaxy!

May the Force be with you,
Leah Parker

SECTION 1

TOYS & AMIGURUMI

"THANK THE MAKER!"

—C-3PO, *Star Wars:* Episode IV—*A New Hope*

From Anakin Skywalker, programmer of the unforgettable C-3PO protocol droid, to Galen Erso, reluctant designer of the Death Star, makers of all stripes populate the *Star Wars* galaxy. These are big endeavours that come from big ideas. As C-3PO says of Anakin in *Star Wars:* Episode II—*Attack of the Clones*, "For a mechanic, you seem to do an incessant amount of thinking." But not every project has to change the fate of the galaxy. Some, like a certain stormtrooper doll created by Galen Erso's wife, Lyra, are intended to bring joy to those around them. And that's a goal worth celebrating, too. In honour of those inventions that bring a bit of light and play to day-to-day life, this section is all about toys and dolls. You'll find patterns ranging from handmade lightsabers to Ewoks to your very own stormtrooper doll. As you take on these projects, don't overthink your work. Instead, endeavour to find the fun in both the making and the finished product!

LIGHTSABERS

Designed by Leah Parker

SKILL LEVEL: ✎

In the *Star Wars* galaxy, any wielder of the Force may use a lightsaber, including the Sith. However, it is most well known as the weapon of a Jedi. And each Jedi is expected to build their own, so they know their lightsaber from the power cell to the casing to the focusing lens to the kyber crystal. It's the crystal that gives each blade its colour, but only when awakened by the Force. While members of the Jedi Order are most often depicted using blue or green lightsabers, the Sith are almost exclusively shown wielding red blades.

Because each Jedi's lightsaber design is unique to its creator, this pattern includes a range of options for you to choose from. Designs can accommodate the preferred hilts of Darth Vader, Luke Skywalker, and Obi-Wan Kenobi. There are also multiple blade colour options, so you can design a lightsaber that's true to you. Just like a Jedi, you're meant to start by working on the hilt first before moving on to your blade. This project may move quickly, but that just means you'll have more time to practice your lightsaber-wielding skills!

> "THIS IS THE WEAPON OF A JEDI KNIGHT. NOT AS CLUMSY OR RANDOM AS A BLASTER. AN ELEGANT WEAPON FOR A MORE CIVILIZED AGE."
>
> —Obi-Wan Kenobi to Luke Skywalker, *A New Hope*

SIZE
One size

FINISHED MEASUREMENTS
Length: approximately 23.5 in. / 60 cm
Circumference: approximately 6.5 in. / 16.5 cm
The circumference of the hilt will vary depending on the details added.

YARN
Worsted weight (medium #4) shown in Lion Brand Yarn *Heartland* (100% Acrylic, 251 yd. / 230 m per 5 oz. / 142 g ball)
Colour A: #136-130R Bryce Canyon, 1 ball
Colour B: #136-152AG White Sands, 1 ball
Colour C: #136-153Q Black Canyon, 1 ball
Colour D: #136-126U Sequoia, 1 ball
Colour E: #136-149R Great Smoky Mountains, 1 ball
Colour F: #136-106AU Voyageurs, 1 ball
Colour G: #136-181E Rocky Mountains, 1 ball
Colour H: #136-113R Redwood, 1 ball

HOOK
D-3 / US 3.25 mm crochet hook, or *size needed to obtain gauge*

NOTIONS
Tapestry needle
Locking stitch markers
Polyester stuffing
Optional: 16-gauge floral wire

GAUGE
12 sts and 12 rnds = 4 in. / 10 cm in sc
Make sure to check your gauge.

PATTERN NOTES
- Stuff Lightsaber as you go.
- Tip: Use a long-handled wooden spoon to pack stuffing. Rolling the Lightsaber on a hard surface will help keep the stuffing even and circular.
- Hilt is worked in joined rounds to help with colour changes.
- Saber is worked continuously in the round without joining.
- Optional: Insert floral wire into the Lightsaber to make it stiffer.

SPECIAL ABBREVIATIONS

- **BOB (4 hdc bobble stitch):** Yarn over (yo), insert hook into indicated stitch, yo and pull up a loop, [yo, insert hook into same stitch, yo and pull up a loop] 3x (9 loops on hook), yo and pull through all loops.

OBI-WAN

Rnd 1: With **A**, 6 sc in a magic ring, join with a sl st in first st – 6 sc.

Rnd 2: Ch 1, 2 sc in each st around, join with a sl st in first st – 12 sc.

Rnd 3: Ch 1, [2 sc in next st, sc in next] around, join with a sl st in first st – 18 sc.

Rnd 4: Ch 1, [2 sc in next st, sc in next 2] around, join with a sl st in first st – 24 sc.

Rnd 5: Ch 1, sc-blo in each st around, join with a sl st in first st.

Rnd 6: Ch 1, sc in each st around, join with a sl st in first st.

Rnd 7: With **B**, ch 1, sc in each st around, join with a sl st in first st.

Rnd 8: Ch 1, sc in each st around, join with a sl st in first st.

Rnd 9: Ch 1, [hdc in next 2 sts, BOB in next 2 sts] around, join with sl st in first st – 12 hdc, 12 bobbles.

When stuffing this section ensure that you push the bobbles out.

Rnd 10: Rep Rnd 9.

Rnds 11–12: Ch 1, sc in each st around, join with a sl st in first st – 24 sc.

Rnds 13–18: With **C**, ch 1, sc in each st around, join with a sl st in first st.

Rnds 19–26: With **B**, ch 1, sc in each st around, join with a sl st in first st.

Rnds 27–36: With **C**, ch 1, sc in each st around, join with a sl st in first st.

Rnds 37–40: With **D**, ch 1, sc in each st around, join with a sl st in first st.

Rnds 41–42: With **C**, ch 1, sc in each st around, join with a sl st in first st.

Rnds 43–48: With **B**, ch 1, sc in each st around, join with a sl st in first st.

Rnds 49: With **F**, ch 1, sc in each st around.

Continue crocheting in rounds without joining until Lightsaber measures approximately 23 in. / 58.5 cm, or desired length.

Next, work [sc2tog in next 2 sts, sc in next] until 8 sts remain. Finish stuffing Lightsaber, then sew the opening closed.

- Tie an approximately 12 in. / 30 cm length of **C** around the transition between Rnds 26 and 27 to create a slight indent in the Hilt.
- Repeat 2 to 3 more times within Rnds 27–36.
- Tie an approximately 12 in. / 30 cm length of **D** tightly within Rnds 37–40, so that the diameter of the Hilt at this point is approximately half that of the rest of the Hilt.

SENSOR DETAIL

Rnd 1: With **C**, 6 sc in a magic ring – 6 sc.

Rnd 2: 2 sc in each st around, join with a sl st in first st – 12 sc.

Fasten off, leaving a long tail for sewing.

Sew onto Rnds 13–18.

ACTIVATION SWITCH

Row 1 (RS): With **B**, ch 9, sc in second ch from hook and in each ch across – 8 sc.

Row 2: Turn, ch 1, sc in each st across.

Rows 3–4: With **A**, turn, ch 1, sc in each st across.

Rows 5–6: With **B**, turn, ch 1, sc in each st across.

Fasten off, leaving a long tail for sewing.

Sew onto Rnds 19–26, slightly to the left of Sensor Detail.

LUKE SKYWALKER

With **B** make a magic ring.

Rnd 1: With **B**, 6 sc in a magic ring, join with a sl st in first st – 6 sc.

Rnd 2: Ch 1, 2 sc in each st around, join with a sl st in first st – 12 sc.

Rnd 3: Ch 1, [2 sc in next st, sc in next] around, join with a sl st in first st – 18 sc.

Rnd 4: Ch 1, [2 sc in next st, sc in next 2] around, join with a sl st in first st – 24 sc.

Rnd 5: Ch 1, sc-blo in each st around, join with a sl st in first st.

Rnd 6–7: Ch 1, sc in each st around, join with a sl st in first st.

Rnd 8: Ch 1, [sc in next 2 sts, BOB in next 2 sts] around, join with sl st in first st – 12 sc, 12 bobbles.

When stuffing this section ensure that you push the bobbles out.

Rnd 9: Ch 1, [hdc in next 2 sts, sc in next 2] around, join with a sl st in first st – 24 sts.

Rnds 10–22: Ch 1, sc in each st around, join with a sl st in first st.

Rnds 23–25: With **C**, ch 1, sc in each st around, join with a sl st in first st.

Rnd 26: With **B**, ch 1, sc in each st around, join with a sl st in first st.

Rnd 27: With **C**, ch 1, sc in each st around, join with a sl st in first st.

Rnds 28–38: Rep Rnds 26–27, ending after a rep of Rnd 26.

Rnds 39–41: With **C**, ch 1, sc in each st around, join with a sl st in first st.

Rnd 42: With **B**, ch 1, sc in each st around, join with a sl st in first st.

Rnds 43–45: With **A**, ch 1, sc in each st around, join with a sl st in first st.

Rnds 46–49: With **B**, ch 1, sc in each st around, join with a sl st in first st.

Rnd 50: With **G**, ch 1, sc in each st around.

Continue crocheting in rounds without joining until Lightsaber measures approximately 25 in. / 63.5 cm, or desired length.

Next, work [sc2tog in next 2 sts] until 6

sts remain. Finish stuffing Lightsaber, then sew the opening closed.

- Tie an approximately 12 in. / 30 cm length of **C** around Rnds 23–25 to create a slight indent in the Hilt.
- Repeat around Rnds 39–41.
- Tie an approximately 12 in. / 30 cm length of **A** tightly within Rnds 43–45, so that the diameter of the Hilt at this point is approximately half that of the rest of the Hilt.

ACTIVATION SWITCH

Row 1 (RS): With **B**, ch 9, sc in second ch from hook and in each ch across – 8 sc.

Row 2: Turn, ch 1, sc in each st across.

Rows 3–4: With **A**, turn, ch 1, sc in each st across.

Rows 5–6: With **B**, turn, ch 1, sc in each st across.

Fasten off, leaving a long tail for sewing.

Sew onto Hilt below Rnd 23.

DARTH VADER

Rnd 1: With **B**, 6 sc in a magic ring, join with a sl st in first st – 6 sc.

Rnd 2: Ch 1, 2 sc in each st around, join with a sl st in first st – 12 sc.

Rnd 3: Ch 1, [2 sc in next, sc in next] around, join with a sl st in first st – 18 sc.

Rnd 4: Ch 1, [2 sc in next, sc in next 2] around, join with a sl st in first st – 24 sc.

Rnd 5: Ch 1, sc-blo in each st around, join with a sl st in first st.

Rnds 6–22: Ch 1, sc in each st around, join with a sl st in first st.

Rnds 23–30: With **C**, ch 1, sc in each st around, join with a sl st in first st.

Rnds 31–40: With **B**, ch 1, sc in each st around, join with a sl st in first st.

Rnds 41–43: With **E**, ch 1, sc in each st around, join with a sl st in first st.

This section will create the Blade Emitter.

Rnd 44: With **E**, ch 1, sc in next 12 sts; with **H**, sc in next 12, join with a sl st in first st.

Rnd 45: Ch 1, sc in first st; with **E**, sc in next 10; with **H**, sc in next 13, join with a sl st in first st.

Rnd 46: Ch 1, sc in first st, sc in next; with **E**, sc in next 8; with **H**, sc in next 14, join with a sl st in first st.

Rnd 47: Ch 1, sc in first st, sc in next 2; with **E**, sc in next 6; with **H**, sc in next 15, join with a sl st in first st.

Rnd 48: Ch 1, sc in first st, sc in next 3; with **E**, sc in next 4; with **H**, sc in next 16, join with a sl st in first st.

Rnd 49: Ch 1, sc in each st around.

Continue crocheting in rounds without joining until Lightsaber measures approximately 25 in. / 63.5 cm, or desired length.

Next, work [sc2tog in next 2 sts] until 6 sts remain. Finish stuffing Lightsaber, then sew the opening closed.

- Tie an approximately 12 in. / 30 cm length of **C** around the transition between Rnds 22 and 23 to create a slight indent in the Hilt.
- Repeat around the transition between Rnds 30 and 31.
- With **B**, repeat around the transition between Rnds 40 and 41.

HANDLE DETAIL (MAKE 6)

Row 1 (RS): With **C**, ch 17, sc in second chain from hook and in each ch across – 16 sc.

Rows 2–3: Ch 1, turn, sc in each st across.

Fasten off, leaving a long tail for sewing.

Pin Handle Details vertically along Rnds 5–22 with RS facing and sew onto Hilt.

ACTIVATION LEVER

Row 1 (RS): With **C**, ch 7, sc in second chain from hook and in each ch across – 6 sc.

Rows 2–4: Ch 1, turn, sc in each st across.

Fasten off, leaving a long tail for sewing.

Sew Activation Lever onto Rnds 23–30 opposite Blade Emitter in Rnds 44–48.

BLADE LEVER

Row 1 (RS): With **C**, ch 9, sc in second chain from hook and in each ch across – 8 sc.

Row 2: Ch 1, turn, sc in each st across.

Fasten off, leaving a long tail for sewing.

Sew Blade Lever onto Blade Emitter, positioning it one third above and two thirds below Rnd 41.

SENSOR DETAIL 1

Rnd 1: With **H**, 6 sc in a magic ring, join with a sl st in first st – 6 sc.

Fasten off, leaving a long tail for sewing.

Sew Sensor Detail 1 approximately 5 sts to the right of the Blade Lever and halfway between Rnds 31–40.

SENSOR DETAIL 2

Rnd 1: With **A**, 6 sc in a magic ring, join with a sl st in first st – 6 sc.

Fasten off, leaving a long tail for sewing.

Sew Sensor Detail 2 above Blade Lever with **E**.

SENSOR DETAIL 3

Rnd 1: With **B**, 6 sc in a magic ring, join with a sl st in first st – 6 sc.

Fasten off, leaving a long tail for sewing.

Sew Sensor Detail 3 onto Blade Lever at Rnd 41.

BELT RING

With **B**, ch 15.

Fasten off. Sew onto Hilt around Sensor Detail 2.

"THIS WEAPON IS YOUR LIFE."

—Obi-Wan Kenobi to Anakin Skywalker, *Star Wars:* Episode II—*Attack of the Clones*

EWOK AMIGURUMI

Designed by Alexis Veenendaal

SKILL LEVEL: ✦ ✦ ✦

Famously curious beings, Ewoks are native to the Forest Moon of Endor and stand about 3½ feet (1 meter) tall. Perhaps it's their unassuming stature or their friendly ways, but whatever the reason may be, the Ewoks are initially overlooked when the Galactic Empire establishes operations on Endor's moon. It's a miscalculation by the Imperials and one that costs them greatly. One brave and adventurous Ewok, Wicket, plays a pivotal role in persuading his tribe to join the Rebel Alliance. Armed only with bows, spears, and their deep knowledge of the forest, they are able to help destroy the shield generator for the second Death Star. Not to be underestimated, the Ewoks are proof that unexpected allies can make all the difference.

If this is your first time crocheting *amigurumi,* a crafting style from Japan that refers to creating small, stuffed figures and toys, then stitching one of the cutest creatures in the galaxy is a great place to start. This pattern is straightforward at first, gradually increasing in complexity as it introduces the Ewoks' classic headscarf and spear. These extra crocheted details will help bring this character to life. And like Wicket, who proves you don't have to be big to make a gigantic impact on your galaxy, this project is a lovable little reminder to not underestimate your own skills. When you're feeling inspired, just say "Yub Nub" to taking a chance!

> "YOU'RE A JITTERY LITTLE THING, AREN'T YOU?"
>
> —Princess Leia,
> *Star Wars*: Episode VI—*Return of the Jedi*

SIZE
One size

FINISHED MEASUREMENTS
Height: 5.5 in. / 14 cm
Width: 3.5 in. / 9 cm

YARN
DK (4-ply) shown in Hobbii *Rainbow Cotton 8/4* (100% Cotton, 175 yd. / 160 m per 1¾ oz. / 50 g ball)
Colour A: #007 Brown - 1 ball
Colour B: #004 Beige - 1 ball
Colour C: #066 Burnt Orange - 1 ball
Colour D: #009 Black - 1 ball
Colour E: #008 Dark Brown - 1 ball
Colour F: #016 Light Grey - 1 ball

HOOK
US C-2 / 2.5 mm crochet hook, or *size needed to obtain gauge*

NOTIONS
Pair of 8 mm black safety eyes
One 9 mm black safety nose
Tapestry needle
Locking stitch markers
Polyester stuffing
Crafting wire (optional)

GAUGE
19 sts and 24 rnds = 4 in. / 10 cm in sc
Make sure to check your gauge.

PATTERN NOTES
- The doll is worked in pieces and assembled.
- Pieces are crocheted in continuous rounds unless otherwise stated.
- The magic ring can be substituted with: Ch 2, 6 sc in second ch from hook.

ABBREVIATIONS
- **Dc popcorn stitch:** Work 5 dc in the same stitch, drop the loop from your hook, then insert the hook from front to back under the top two loops of the first double crochet. Hook the dropped loop and pull it through the stitch.
- **Inv dec (invisible decrease):** Insert hook into the front loop of the next 2 sts, yarn over and draw through two loops, yarn over and draw through remaining loops.

TOYS & AMIGURUMI

HEAD

Stuff Head as you go. Be careful not to overstuff the Head, or the Head Scarf might not fit. You can choose to make the Head Scarf first, then see how much stuffing you need based on that.

Rnd 1: With **A**, 6 sc in a magic ring – 6 sts.

Rnd 2: 2 sc in each st around – 12 sts.

Rnd 3: [Sc in next st, 2 sc in next] around – 18 sts.

Rnd 4: [Sc in next 2 sts, 2 sc in next] around – 24 sts.

Rnd 5: [Sc in next 3 sts, 2 sc in next] around – 30 sts.

Rnd 6: [Sc in next 4 sts, 2 sc in next] around – 36 sts.

Rnd 7: [Sc in next 5 sts, 2 sc in next] around – 42 sts.

Rnd 8: [Sc in next 6 sts, 2 sc in next] around – 48 sts.

Rnd 9: [Sc in next 7 sts, 2 sc in next] around – 54 sts.

Rnd 10: [Sc in next 8 sts, 2 sc in next] around – 60 sts.

Rnd 11: [Sc in next 9 sts, 2 sc in next] x2, sc in next 20 sts, [sc in next 9 sts, 2 sc in next] x2 – 64 sts.

Rnds 12–22: Sc in each st around.

Rnd 23: [Sc in next 9 sts, inv dec] x2, sc in next 20 sts, [sc in next 9 sts, inv dec] x2 – 60 sts.

Rnd 24: [Sc in next 8 sts, inv dec] around – 54 sts.

Rnd 25: [Sc in next 7 sts, inv dec] around – 48 sts.

Rnd 26: [Sc in next 6 sts, inv dec] around – 42 sts.

Rnd 27: [Sc in next 5 sts, inv dec] around – 36 sts.

Do not fasten off. Continue to Body.

BODY

Alternating between **A** and **B**.

Rnd 28: With **A**, [sc in next 11 sts, 2 sc in next] around – 39 sts.

Rnd 29: Sc in next 5 sts, 2 sc in next, sc in next 12, 2 sc in next, sc in next 6; with **B**, sc in next 8; with **A**, 2 sc in next, sc in next 5 – 42 sts.

Rnd 30: Sc in next 13 sts, 2 sc in next, sc in next 13; with **B**, 2 sc in next, sc in next 6, 2 sc in next; with **A**, sc in next 7 – 45 sts.

Rnd 31: Sc in next 28 sts; with **B**, sc in next 10; with **A**, sc in next 7 – 45 sts.

Add Safety Eyes between Rnds 16 and 17 with 9 to 10 sts between them.

Centre the Nose between the Eyes, 2 rnds below. Make sure the Nose is also centred with the belly.

Rnd 32: Sc in next 6 sts, 2 sc in next, sc in next 20; with **B**, 2 sc in next, sc in next 8, 2 sc in next; with **A**, 8 sc in next – 48 sts.

Rnd 33: Sc in next 28 sts; with **B**, sc in next 12; with **A**, sc in next 8 – 48 sts.

Rnd 34: Sc in next 27 sts; with **B**, sc in next 14; with **A**, sc in next 7 – 48 sts.

Rnds 35–36: Sc in next 27 sts; with **B**, sc in next 14; with **A**, sc in next 7 – 48 sts.

Rnd 37: Sc in next 25 sts; with **B**, sc in next 16 sts; with **A**, sc in next 7 – 48 sts.

Rnd 38: Sc in next 6 sts, inv dec, sc in next 18; with **B**, inv dec, sc in next 12 sts, inv dec; with **A**, sc in next 6 – 45 sts.

Rnd 39: Sc in next 12 sts, inv dec, sc in next 10; with **B**, inv dec, sc in next 10, inv dec; with **A**, sc in next 7 – 42 sts.

Cut **B** and continue with **A**.

BEHIND THE SCENES

The word *Ewok* is never spoken in *Return of the Jedi*, the film where these fan-favourite figures make their first appearance.

Rnd 40: [Sc in next 5 sts, inv dec] around – 36 sts.

Rnd 41: [Sc in next 4 sts, inv dec] around – 30 sts.

Rnd 42: [Sc in next 3 sts, inv dec] around – 24 sts.

Rnd 43: [Sc in next 2 sts, inv dec] around – 18 sts.

Rnd 44: [Sc in next st, inv dec] around – 12 sts.

Rnd 45: [Inv dec] around – 6 sts.

Fasten off.

LEGS (MAKE 2)

Rnd 1: With **B**, 6 sc in a magic ring – 6 sts.

Rnd 2: 2 sc in each st around – 12 sts.

Rnd 3: [Sc in next st, 2 sc in next] around – 18 sts.

Rnd 4: Sc in each st around – 18 sts.

Rnd 5: Sc in next 5 sts, [inv dec] x4, sc in next 5 – 14 sts.

Now working in rows.

Row 6: Sc in next 5 sts, ch 1, turn – 5 sts.

Rows 7–9: Sc in next 11 sts, ch 1, turn – 11 sts.

Row 10: Sc in next st, sc2tog x5, ch 1, turn – 6 sts.

Row 11: Sc2tog x3, ch 1, turn – 3 sts.

Row 12: Sc3tog – 1 st. Do not turn.

Now working in rounds.

Rnd 13: Sc 4 evenly in row ends, sc in next 8 sts, sc 3 evenly in row ends, sc in next – 16 sts.

Rnd 14: Sc in each st around – 16 sts.

Rnd 15: Sc in next 3 sts, 2 sc in next, sc in next 8, 2 sc in next, sc in next 3 – 18 sts.

RIGHT LEG

Rnd 16: Sc in next 11 sts, hdc in next, dc in next 4, hdc in next, sc in next – 18 sts.

Rnd 17: Sl st in next 10 sts, sc in next, hdc in next 6, sc in next – 18 sts.

Fasten off, leaving a long tail for sewing.

Sew Toe details in beige yarn.

LEFT LEG

Rnd 16: Sc in next st, hdc in next, dc in next 4, hdc in next, 11 sc in next – 18 sts.

Rnd 17: Sc in next st, hdc in next 6, sc in next, sl st in next 10 – 18 sts.

Fasten off, leaving a long tail for sewing.

Sew Toe details in beige yarn.

OUTER EAR (MAKE 2)

Rnd 1: With **A**, 6 sc in a magic ring – 6 sts.

Rnd 2: 2 sc in each st around – 12 sts.

Rnd 3: [Sc in next st, 2 sc in next] around – 18 sts.

Rnds 4–6: Sc in each st around.

Fasten off, leaving a long tail for sewing.

INNER EAR (MAKE 2)

Row 1: With **B**, ch 6, sc in second ch from hook, hdc in next 3, sc in next, turn – 5 sts.

Row 2: Sl st in next, hdc in next, dc in next, hdc in next, sl st in next – 5 sts.

Fasten off, leaving a long tail for sewing.

ARMS (MAKE 2)

Rnd 1: With **A**, 5 sc in a magic ring – 5 sts.

Rnd 2: 2 sc in each st around – 10 sts.

Rnds 3–4: Sc in each st around.

Rnd 5 (Left Arm only): Popcorn in first st, sc in next 9 – 10 sts.

Rnd 5 (Right Arm only): Sc in next 9 sts, popcorn in next – 10 sts.

Rnds 6–13: Sc in each st around – 10 sts.

Stuff lightly, crochet across to flatten, sewing both sides together with 5 sc.

Fasten off, leaving a long tail for sewing.

HEAD SCARF

Rnd 1: With **C**, 6 sc in a magic ring – 6 sts.

Rnd 2: 2 hdc in each st around – 12 sts.

Rnd 3: [Hdc in next st, 2 hdc in next] around – 18 sts.

Rnd 4: [Hdc in next 2 sts, 2 hdc in next] around – 24 sts.

Rnd 5: [Hdc in next 3 sts, 2 hdc in next] around – 30 sts.

Rnd 6: [Hdc in next 4 sts, 2 hdc in next] around – 36 sts.

Rnd 7: [Hdc in next 5 sts, 2 hdc in next] around – 42 sts.

Rnd 8: [Hdc in next 6 sts, 2 hdc in next] around – 48 sts.

Rnd 9: [Hdc in next 7 sts, 2 hdc in next] around – 54 sts.

Now working in rows.

Row 10: Hdc in next 14 sts, ch 8 (Ear opening), skip 8, hdc in next 4, ch 8 (Ear opening), sk 8, hdc in next 14, ch 1, turn, leaving remaining sts unworked – 48 sts.

Rows 11–14: Hdc in each st across, ch 1, turn.

Row 15: Hdc in each st across.

FRONT OF HOOD

Row 16: Ch 1, turn, sc in next 12 sts – 12 sts.

Row 17: Ch 1, turn, sc in next 10 sts, sc2tog – 11 sts.

Row 18: Ch 1, turn, sc2tog, sc in next 9 – 10 sts.

Row 19: Ch 1, turn, sc in next 8 sts, sc2tog – 9 sts.

Row 20: Ch 1, turn, sc2tog, sc in next 7 – 8 sts.

Row 21: Ch 1, turn, sc in next 6 sts, sc2tog – 7 sts.

Row 22: Ch 1, turn, sc2tog, sc in next 5 – 6 sts.

Rows 23–32: Ch 1, turn, sc in next 6 sts – 6 sts.

Row 33: Ch 1, turn, sc in next 5 sts, 2 sc in next, ch 1, turn – 7 sts.

Row 34: 2 sc in next st, sc in next 6 sts, ch 1, turn – 8 sts.

Row 35: Sc in next 7 sts, 2 sc in next, ch 1, turn – 9 sts.

Row 36: 2 sc in next st, sc in next 8 sts, ch 1, turn – 10 sts.

Row 37: Sc in next 9 sts, 2 sc in next, ch 1, turn – 11 sts.

Row 38: Sc2tog, sc in next 9, ch 1, turn – 10 sts.

Row 39: Sc in next 8 sts, sc2tog – 9 sts.

Now working around Hood.

Last rnd: Ch 1, sc around entire Hood for a neater edge – approximately 113 sts.

Fasten off, leaving a long tail for sewing. *Front of Hood will be sewn at Assembly.*

TAIL

Rnd 1: With **A**, 5 sc in a magic ring – 5 sts.

Rnd 2: [Sc in next st, 2 sc in next] x2, sc in next – 7 sts.

Rnds 3–4: Sc in each st around.

Fasten off, leaving a long tail for sewing.

SPEAR

SHAFT

Rnd 1: With **E**, 4 sc in a magic ring – 4 sts.

Rnds 2–31: Sc in each st around.

Fasten off, weave ends in.

SPEAR TIP

Rnd 1: With **F**, 3 sc in a magic ring – 3 sts.

Rnd 2: Sc in each st around.

Rnd 3: 2 sc in each st around – 6 sts.

Rnd 4: [2 sc in next st, sc in next 2] x2 – 8 sts.

Rnd 5: [2 sc in next st, sc in next 3] x2 – 10 sts.

Fasten off, leaving a long tail for sewing.

ASSEMBLY

Ears: Fold the Outer Ear in half. Then, pin the Inner Ear onto the front half of the Outer Ear and sew in place, aligning the Ears with the top holes of the Head Scarf.

Tail: Pin Tail to the back of the Ewok, just above the Legs and sew in place.

Details: With **B**, embroider Eyebrows and Whiskers.

Legs and Arms: Attach Legs to the bottom of the Body, Feet facing forward. Ensure the bulky side of Legs faces the outside of the doll. Attach the Arms to the Body below the Neck.

Once the Head Scarf is in place, sew front in place to cover the Ewok's face.

Optional: Embroider a Mouth as a line with **D**.

Spear: Centre the Spear Tip on top of the Shaft and sew in place.

Insert craft wire through the centre of the Spear.

JAWA AMIGURUMI

Designed by Alexis Veenendaal

SKILL LEVEL: ///

The official appearance of the Jawas, underneath their hoods, has not been confirmed. However, George Lucas did create an initial prototype that resembled a rat, which he decided to scrap before filming.

Native to the Outer Rim world of Tatooine, Jawas are skilled scavengers who comb the deserts for scraps and even full droids that they can sell, swap, or trade. They have a reputation for passing off roughly refurbished equipment and have even been accused of swindling their customers. Jawas typically travel over dunes using their sandcrawler transports, which double as mobile bases or fortresses. They've been known to circulate near podracing tracks, looking for opportunities to gather up useful debris after crashes. Clever and resourceful, if not always considered "aboveboard" in their transactions, the *Star Wars* films would not be the same without them. In fact, it's the Jawas who sell C-3PO and R2-D2 to Owen Lars, Luke Skywalker's uncle.

If you're in the mood to take some cues from the Jawas, you can apply some crafty ingenuity to crocheting this sweet amigurumi. Just as they piece together their findings into something new, you will crochet each part separately and then sew them all together. Unlike a Jawa project, however, there's no need for haste. Follow these step-by-step instructions in your own time and you'll ensure your project is assembled to perfection!

"I CAN'T ABIDE THOSE JAWAS!"

—C-3PO, *Star Wars: Episode IV—A New Hope*

SIZE
One size

FINISHED MEASUREMENTS
Height: 5.5 in. / 14 cm
Width: 3.5 in. / 9 cm

YARN
DK (4-ply) shown in Hobbii *Rainbow Cotton 8/4* (100% Cotton, 175 yd. / 160 m per 1¾ oz. / 50 g ball)
Colour A: #009 Black, 1 ball
Colour B: #008 Dark Brown, 1 ball
Colour C: #007 Light Brown, 1 ball
Colour D: #055 Sunny Yellow, 1 ball
Colour E: #006 Brown, 1 ball

HOOK
US C-2 / 2.5 mm crochet hook, or *size needed to obtain gauge*

NOTIONS
Tapestry needle
Locking stitch markers
Polyester stuffing

GAUGE
19 sts and 24 rnds = 4 in. / 10 cm in sc
Make sure to check your gauge.

PATTERN NOTES
- The doll is worked in pieces and assembled.
- Pieces are crocheted in continuous rounds unless otherwise stated.
- The magic ring can be substituted with: (Ch 2, 6 sc) in second ch from hook.

ABBREVIATIONS
- **Inv dec (invisible decrease):** Insert hook into the front loop of the next 2 sts, yarn over and draw through two loops, yarn over and draw through remaining loops.
- **Popcorn:** Work 5 dc in the same st, drop loop from hook, insert hook from front to back in first dc. Put dropped loop back on hook and pull it through the st.

HEAD

Rnd 1: With **A**, 6 sc in a magic ring – 6 sts.

Rnd 2: 2 sc in each st around – 12 sts.

Rnd 3: [Sc in next st, 2 sc in next] around – 18 sts.

Rnd 4: [Sc in next 2 sts, 2 sc in next] around – 24 sts.

Rnd 5: [Sc in next 3 sts, 2 sc in next] around – 30 sts.

Rnd 6: [Sc in next 4 sts, 2 sc in next] around – 36 sts.

Rnd 7: [Sc in next 5 sts, 2 sc in next] around – 42 sts.

Rnd 8: [Sc in next 6 sts, 2 sc in next] around – 48 sts.

Rnd 9: [Sc in next 7 sts, 2 sc in next] around – 54 sts.

Rnd 10: [Sc in next 8 sts, 2 sc in next] around – 60 sts.

Rnds 11–22: Sc in each st around.

Stuff the Head as you go.

Rnd 23: [Sc in next 8 sts, inv dec] around – 54 sts.

Rnd 24: [Sc in next 7 sts, inv dec] around – 48 sts.

Rnd 25: [Sc in next 6 sts, inv dec] around – 42 sts.

Rnd 26: [Sc in next 5 sts, inv dec] around – 36 sts.

Rnd 27: [Sc in next 4 sts, inv dec] around – 30 sts.

Rnd 28: [Sc in next 3 sts, inv dec] around – 24 sts.

Rnd 29: [Sc in next 2 sts, inv dec] around – 18 sts.

Rnd 30: [Sc in next st, inv dec] around – 12 sts.

Rnd 31: [Inv dec] around – 6 sts.

Fasten off.

EYES (MAKE 2)

Rnd 1: With **D**, 5 sc in a magic ring – 5 sts.

Fasten off, leaving a long tail for sewing.

Sew Eyes to Head between Rnds 18 and 19, with 8 or 9 sts between them.

LEGS (MAKE 2)

RIGHT LEG

Rnd 1: With **B**, 6 sc in a magic ring – 6 sts.

Rnd 2: 2 sc in each st around – 12 sts.

Rnd 3: [Sc in next st, 2 sc in next] around – 18 sts.

Rnd 4: [Sc in next 2 sts, 2 sc in next] around – 24 sts.

Rnd 5: Sc-blo in each st around.

Rnd 6: Sc in each st around.

Rnd 7: Sc in next 6 sts, [inv dec] x6, sc in next 6 sts – 18 sts.

Rnd 8: Sc in next 6 sts, [inv dec] x3, sc in next 6 sts – 15 sts.

Rnd 9: Sc in next 7 sts, inv dec, sc in next 6 sts – 14 sts.

Fasten off and weave ends in. Start stuffing the Leg.

LEFT LEG

Repeat Right Leg (Rnds 1–9) but instead of cutting the yarn, join the Legs and continue with the Body. If needed, continue in sc to reach the centre of the side of the Leg.

Ch 3, join Left Leg to Right Leg.

Round 10: Sc in 14 sc around Right Leg, sc in 3 chs, sc in 14 sc around Left Leg, sc in 3 chs – 34 sts.

Add stitch marker at the end of this round to mark your new starting point. Do not cut yarn and continue to the Body.

BODY

Stuff Body as you go.

Rnds 11–12: With **B**, sc in each st around – 34 sts.

Rnd 13: [Sc in next 15 sts, inv dec] x2 – 32 sts.

Rnd 14. Sc in each st around – 32 sts.

Rnd 15: [Sc in next 14 sts, inv dec] x2 – 30 sts.

Rnd 16: Sc in each st around.

Rnd 17: [Sc in next 13 sts, inv dec] x2 – 28 sts.

Rnd 18: Sc in each st around.

Rnd 19: [Sc in next 12 sts, inv dec] x2 – 26 sts.

Rnd 20: Sc in each st around.

Rnd 21: [Sc in next 11 sts, inv dec] x2 – 24 sts.

Rnd 22: Sc in each st around.

Rnd 23: [Sc in next 10 sts, inv dec] x2 – 22 sts.

Rnd 24: Sc-blo in each st around.

Fasten off, leaving a long tail for sewing.

ROBE

Rnd 1: With Body facing down, attach **C** to an unused loop from Rnd 23 at the back of the Body. Ch 2 (does not count as a st in this section), hdc in next 22 sts, sl st in first st, ch 2, turn – 22 sts.

Rnd 2: [Hdc in next 10 sts, 2 hdc in next] x2, sl st in first stitch, ch 2, turn – 24 sts.

Rnd 3: [Hdc in next 3 sts, 2 hdc in next] x6, sl st in first stitch, ch 2, turn – 30 sts.

Rnds 4–6: Hdc in each st around, sl st in first stitch, ch 2, turn.

Rnd 7: [Hdc in next 4 sts, 2 hdc in next] x6, sl st in first stitch, sl st in first stitch, ch 2, turn – 36 sts.

Rnd 8: Hdc in each st around, ch 2, turn.

Rnd 9: Hdc in each st around,

sl st in first stitch, Fasten off.

ARMS (MAKE 2)

Rnd 1: With **B**, 5 sc in a magic ring – 5 sts.

Rnd 2: 2 sc in each st around – 10 sts.

Rnd 3: Sc in each st around.

Rnd 4: Sc in next st, popcorn in next st, sc in next 8 sts – 10 sts.

Rnd 5: Sc in each st around.

Rnds 6–10: With **C**, sc in each st around.

Rnd 11: Sc-blo in each st around.

Stuff lightly, crochet across to flatten, sewing both sides together with 5 sc.

Fasten off.

SLEEVES (MAKE 2)

Attach **C** to Rnd 11 of Arm, with the Hand facing down.

Rnd 1: Ch 1, sc in each st around – 10 sts.

Rnd 2: [Sc in next st, 2 sc in next] x5 – 15 sts.

Rnd 3: Sc in each st around. 15 sts.

Rnd 4: [Sc in next 4 sts, 2 sc in next] x3 – 18 sts.

Rnds 5–7: Sc in each st around.

Fasten off.

HOOD

Rnd 1: With **C**, 6 sc in a magic ring – 6 sts.

Rnd 2: 2 hdc in each st around – 12 sts.

Rnd 3: [Hdc in next st, 2 hdc in next] around – 18 sts.

Rnd 4: [Hdc in next 2 sts, 2 hdc in next] around – 24 sts.

Rnd 5: [Hdc in next 3 sts, 2 hdc in next] around – 30 sts.

Rnd 6: [Hdc in next 4 sts, 2 hdc in next] around – 36 sts.

Rnd 7: [Hdc in next 5 sts, 2 hdc in next] around – 42 sts.

Rnd 8: [Hdc in next 6 sts, 2 hdc in next] around – 48 sts.

Rnd 9: [Hdc in next 7 sts, 2 hdc in next] around – 54 sts.

Rnd 10: [Hdc in next 8 sts, 2 hdc in next] around – 60 sts.

Rnd 11: [Hdc in next 9 sts, 2 hdc in next] around – 66 sts.

Rnd 12: Hdc in each st around.

Now working in rows.

Rows 13–15: Hdc in next 55 sts, ch 1, turn – 55 sts.

Row 16: Hdc in each st across.

Row 17: Ch 3, turn, starting in second ch, hdc in next 2 chs, hdc in next 55 hdc, ch 3, turn – 57 sts.

Row 18: Starting in second ch, hdc in next 2 chs, hdc in next 57 hdc, ch 2, turn – 59 sts.

Row 19: Starting in second ch, hdc in next ch, hdc in next 59 hdc, ch 1, turn – 60 sts.

Row 20: Working evenly around hood, sc in next 60 hdc, ch 1, 9 sc in row ends, 13 sc across front of Hood, 9 sc in row ends, sl st in first st. Stitch count is not crucial here.

Fasten off, leaving a long tail for sewing.

LARGE SASH

Row 1: With **B**, ch 41, sc in second ch from hook and in each ch across – 40 sts.

Fold in half and twist once, then sew short ends together to form a loop. Fasten off, weave in ends and slip onto Jawa.

SMALL SASH

Row 1: With **E**, ch 36, sc in second ch from hook and in each ch across – 35 sts.

Fold in half and twist once as per Small Sash, sew short ends together, fasten off and weave in ends. Slip onto Jawa in the other direction, so your sashes cross each other.

Optional: Sew the Sashes onto the Shoulder.

Optional: Add Sash details (lines embroidered with **C** or the colour of your choice).

ASSEMBLY

Align and pin the Head onto the Body, then sew in place.

Pin the Arms to both sides of the Body, aligned with the outside of each Leg, and sew to the Neck (Rnd 24).

Wrap the Hood over the Head so the flat edge is centred over the back of the Neck. Then squeeze the ends together under the Jawa's Neck, pin everything in place, and sew Hood to Body around neckline.

TOYS & AMIGURUMI 25

MACE WINDU AMIGURUMI

Designed by Alexis Veenendaal

SKILL LEVEL: ✦✦✦

Mace Windu is a Jedi Master and member of the High Council during the final years of the Galactic Republic. He is revered as one of the most powerful Jedi of his time and easily recognizable on the battlefield due to his purple lightsaber. Initially, he opposes the idea of Anakin Skywalker training as a Jedi and, later, of joining the ranks of Jedi Masters.

Over time, Windu also becomes increasingly suspicious of Chancellor Palpatine, sensing a corresponding change in the Force as Palpatine, and the dark side, become more powerful. However, it's Anakin Skywalker who helps confirm Mace Windu's suspicions, uncovering Palpatine's secret identity as Darth Sidious. But the confrontation between Windu and Palpatine leads Anakin to intervene, saving the chancellor's life and betraying Windu in the process. In the end, Windu's concerns about both men prove justified, if in unexpected ways.

In honour of the powerful Jedi Master, crochet this amigurumi version of Mace Windu with confidence. Trust the pattern, your instincts as a crafter, and Mace Windu himself. This project is worked continuously in the round, a technique as seamless as the Jedi's focus on the battlefield. And speaking of battles, don't forget to crochet Windu's tiny purple lightsaber. When you're done, you may have just the leader your amigurumi collection needs!

"YOU REFER TO THE PROPHECY OF THE ONE WHO WILL BRING BALANCE TO THE FORCE. YOU BELIEVE IT'S THIS BOY?"

—Mace Windu, *Star Wars: Episode I—The Phantom Menace*

SIZE
One size

FINISHED MEASUREMENTS
Height: 7 in. / 18 cm
Width: 4 in. / 10 cm

YARN
DK (4-ply) shown in Hobbii *Rainbow Cotton 8/4* (100% Cotton, 175 yd. / 160 m per 1¾ oz. / 50 g ball)
Colour A: #007 Brown, 1 ball
Colour B: #006 Light Brown, 1 ball
Colour C: #004 Beige, 1 ball
Colour D: #011 Dark Grey, 1 ball
Colour E: #037 Dark Purple, 1 ball
Colour F: #016 Light Grey, 1 ball
Colour G: #009 Black, 1 ball

HOOK
US C-2 / 2.5 mm crochet hook, or *size needed to obtain gauge*

NOTIONS
Pair of 8 mm black safety eyes
Tapestry needle
Locking stitch marker
Polyester stuffing
Crafting wire (optional)

GAUGE
19 sts and 24 rnds = 4 in. / 10 cm in sc
Make sure to check your gauge.

PATTERN NOTES
- The doll is worked in pieces and assembled.
- Pieces are crocheted in continuous rounds unless otherwise stated.
- The magic ring can be substituted with: Ch 2, 6 sc in second ch from hook.

SPECIAL ABBREVIATIONS
- **Inv dec (invisible decrease):** Insert hook into the front loop of the next 2 sts, yarn over and draw through two loops, yarn over and draw through remaining loops.
- **Popcorn:** Work 5 dc in the same st, drop loop from hook, insert hook from front to back in first dc. Put dropped loop back on hook and pull it through the st.

HEAD

Rnd 1: With **A**, 6 sc in a magic ring – 6 sts.

Rnd 2: 2 sc in each st around – 12 sts.

Rnd 3: [Sc in next st, 2 sc in next] around – 18 sts.

Rnd 4: [Sc in next 2 sts, 2 sc in next] around – 24 sts.

Rnd 5: [Sc in next 3 sts, 2 sc in next] around – 30 sts.

Rnd 6: [Sc in next 4 sts, 2 sc in next] around – 36 sts.

Rnd 7: [Sc in next 5 sts, 2 sc in next] around – 42 sts.

Rnd 8: [Sc in next 6 sts, 2 sc in next] around – 48 sts.

Rnd 9: [Sc in next 7 sts, 2 sc in next] around – 54 sts.

Rnd 10: [Sc in next 8 sts, 2 sc in next] around – 60 sts.

Rnds 11–22: Sc in each st around.

Add Safety Eyes in Rnd 18 with 10 sts between them.

Stuff the Head as you go.

Rnd 23: [Sc in next 8 sts, inv dec] around – 54 sts.

Rnd 24: [Sc in next 7 sts, inv dec] around – 48 sts.

Rnd 25: [Sc in next 6 sts, inv dec] around – 42 sts.

Rnd 26: [Sc in next 5 sts, inv dec] around – 36 sts.

Rnd 27: [Sc in next 4 sts, inv dec] around – 30 sts.

Rnd 28: [Sc in next 3 sts, inv dec] around – 24 sts.

Rnd 29: [Sc in next 2 sts, inv dec] around – 18 sts.

Rnd 30: [Sc in next st, inv dec] around – 12 sts.

Rnd 31: [Inv dec] around – 6 sts.

Fasten off.

EAR (MAKE 2)

Row 1: With **A**, 5 hdc in a magic ring – 5 sts.

Row 2: Ch 1, turn, sc in next 5 sts.

Fasten off.

LEG (MAKE 2)

RIGHT LEG

Rnd 1: With **B**, 6 sc in a magic ring – 6 sts.

Rnd 2: 2 sc in each st around – 12 sts.

Rnd 3: [Sc in next st, 2 sc in next] around – 18 sts.

Rnd 4: [Sc in next 2 sts, 2 sc in next] around – 24 sts.

Rnd 5: Sc-blo in each st around.

Rnd 6: Sc in each st around.

Rnd 7: Sc in next 6 sts, [inv dec] x6, sc in next 6 sts – 18 sts.

Rnd 8: Sc in next 6 sts, [inv dec] x3, sc in next 6 sts – 15 sts.

Rnds 9–11: Sc in each st around.

Rnd 12: With **C**, sc-blo in each st around.

Rnds 13–15: Sc in each st around.

Fasten off and weave in ends. Start stuffing the Leg.

LEFT LEG

Repeat Right Leg (Rnds 1–15), but instead of cutting the yarn, join the Legs and continue with the Body.

JOIN THE LEGS

Rnd 16: Sc in 13 sc on Left Leg, ch 3, join to Right Leg (connecting the insides so the Feet face forward), 15 sc working clockwise around Right Leg – 31 sts.

Add a stitch marker at the end of this round to mark your new starting point. Do not cut yarn.

BEHIND THE SCENES

On-screen, Mace Windu wields a purple lightsaber. This was a request from Samuel L. Jackson, the actor who plays Windu. Purple is Jackson's favourite colour.

BODY

Stuff Body as you go.

Rnd 17: With **C**, [sc in next 3 chs, sc in next 15 sc] 2x – 36 sts.

Rnds 18–19: Sc in each st around.

Rnd 20: [Sc in next 16 sts, inv dec] x2 – 34 sts.

Rnd 21: Sc in each st around.

Rnd 22: [Sc in next 15 sts, inv dec] x2 – 32 sts.

Rnd 23: Sc in each st around.

Rnd 24: With **B**, working in blo [sc in next 14 sts, inv dec] x2 – 30 sts.

Rnd 25: Sc in each st around.

Rnd 26: With **D**, working in blo [sc in next 13 sts, inv dec] x2 – 28 sts.

Rnd 27: Sc in each st around.

Rnd 28: [Sc in next 12 sts, inv dec] x2 – 26 sts.

Rnd 29: Sc in each st around.

Now alternating between **D** and **C**.

Make sure this section is centred. If it is not, shift **D** slightly by making a few sts so your first **C** st sits in the centre front of the torso.

Tip: For a neater look, work **C** sts in the front loop only.

Rnd 30: With **D**, sc in next 11 sts, inv dec, sc in next 5; with **C**, sc in next; with **D**, sc in next 5, inv dec – 24 sts.

Rnd 31: With **D**, sc in next 16 sts; with **C**, sc in next 3; with **D**, sc in next 5 – 24 sts.

Rnd 32: With **D**, sc in next 10 sts, inv dec, sc in next 4; with **C**, sc in next 4; with **D**, sc in next 2, inv dec – 22 sts.

Rnd 33: With **D**, sc in next 15 sts; with **C**, sc in next 5; with **D**, sc in next 2 – 22 sts.

Fasten off, leaving a long tail for sewing.

ROBE

With Head facing down, join **D** to the unworked front loops at Rnd 23. Attach yarn at the centre front of the Body, aligned with the centre of the Legs.

TOYS & AMIGURUMI 29

Rnd 1: Ch 2 (does not count as first st in this section), hdc in next 32 sts, sl st to first st – 32 sts.

Rnds 2–3: Ch 2, hdc in next 32 sts, sl st to first st – 32 sts.

Now, we'll be splitting the Robe.

Rnd 4: Ch 2, turn, hdc in next 31 sts, sl st in next – 31 sts.

Rnd 5: Ch 2, turn, hdc in each st across.

Now working around the entire bottom of the Robe for a neater finish:

Rnd 6: Ch 1, work 6 sl sts into dip in the front of the robe, ch 1, sl st in each st around, sl st in first sl st – 37 sts.

Fasten off.

ARMS (MAKE 2)

Rnd 1: With **A**, 5 sc in a magic ring – 5 sts.

Rnd 2: 2 sc in each st around – 10 sts.

Rnd 3: Sc in each st around.

Rnd 4: Sc in next st, popcorn in next, sc in next 8 sts – 10 sts.

Rnd 5: Sc in each st around.

Rnd 6: With **D**, sc in each st around.

Rnd 7: Sc-blo in each st around.

Rnds 8–15: Sc in each st around.

Stuff lightly. Crochet across to flatten, sewing both sides together with 5 sc.

Fasten off.

SLEEVE CUFF

Attach **D** to unworked loops at Rnd 7, with Hand facing down.

Rnd 1: Ch 1, hdc in next 10 sts, sl st in first st – 10 sts.

Fasten off.

LIGHTSABER

Rnd 1: With **F**, 5 sc in a magic ring – 5 sts.

Rnd 2: Sc in each st around.

Rnd 3: Sc-blo in each st around.

Rnds 4–6: Sc in each st around.

Rnd 7: With **E**, sc-blo in each st around.

Rnds 8–26: Sc in each st around.

Fasten off and weave tail through 5 sts. Pull tight to close and weave in ends.

ASSEMBLY

Align and pin the Head onto the Body, then sew in place.

Pin the Arms to both sides of the Body, aligned with the outside of both Legs, and sew to the Body (Rnd 33).

Attach the Ears 6 sts from the outside of each Eye and in line with the Eyes.

DETAILS

With **G** or black thread, embroider the Eyebrows.

With **A**, embroider the Nose centred between the Eyes, 2–3 sts wide.

With **D** and **G**, embroider details on the Handle of the Lightsaber.

Sew details across the front of the Robe with **D** to create neckline (see pictures for reference).

Optional: Sew the Lightsaber to Mace Windu's Hand using **A**, looping it around the Handle.

Optional: Cut a straight piece of crafting wire and insert it through the centre of the Lightsaber to keep it in place.

MACE WINDU: "THERE'S NO DOUBT THE MYSTERIOUS WARRIOR WAS A SITH."
YODA: "ALWAYS TWO, THERE ARE. NO MORE, NO LESS. A MASTER AND AN APPRENTICE."
MACE WINDU: "BUT WHICH WAS DESTROYED, THE MASTER OR THE APPRENTICE?"

—*The Phantom Menace*

LANDO CALRISSIAN AMIGURUMI

Designed by Alexis Veenendaal

SKILL LEVEL: ///

Lando Calrissian was the owner of the *Millennium Falcon*; that is, until he lost it to Han Solo in a game of sabacc. A former smuggler like Solo, Calrissian eventually becomes the leader of a floating mining colony known as Cloud City. There, he is pressured by Darth Vader to draw a group of rebels, including Han Solo and Princess Leia, straight into the hands of the Empire. But when Darth Vader alters the terms of the deal, endangering Han Solo's life, Calrissian decides to join the Rebel Alliance himself.

While Lando Calrissian may have started off causing trouble for the Rebellion, he becomes an integral part of their victory during the Battle of Endor. Piloting his old freighter, the *Millennium Falcon*, he fires the iconic shot into the core of the Death Star II, destroying the battle station. If you're looking for a straightforward and reliable pattern, with no tricks, try out these instructions to create your very own Lando! This project is not only worked piece by piece but also stuffed as you go, ensuring your amigurumi captures every detail of this smooth-talking rebel hero.

"WHY YOU SLIMY, DOUBLE-CROSSING, NO-GOOD SWINDLER. YOU'VE GOT A LOT OF GUTS COMING HERE, AFTER WHAT YOU PULLED."

—Lando Calrissian to Han Solo, *Star Wars: Episode V—The Empire Strikes Back*

SIZE
One size

FINISHED MEASUREMENTS
Height: 7 in. / 18 cm
Width: 4 in. / 10 cm

YARN
DK (4-ply) shown in Hobbii *Rainbow Cotton 8/4* (100% Cotton, 175 yd. / 160 m per 1¾ oz. / 50 g ball)
Colour A: #006 Light Brown, 1 ball
Colour B: #007 Brown, 1 ball
Colour C: #011 Dark Grey, 1 ball
Colour D: #030 Navy Blue, 1 ball
Colour E: #033 Turquoise, 1 ball
Colour F: #009 Black, 1 ball

HOOK
US C-2 / 2.5 mm crochet hook, or *size needed to obtain gauge*

NOTIONS
Pair of 8 mm black safety eyes
Tapestry needle
Locking stitch markers
Polyester stuffing

GAUGE
19 sts and 24 rnds = 4 in. / 10 cm in sc
Make sure to check your gauge.

PATTERN NOTES
- The doll is worked in pieces and assembled.
- Pieces are crocheted in continuous rounds unless otherwise stated.
- The magic ring can be substituted with: Ch 2, 6 sc in second ch from hook.

SPECIAL ABBREVIATIONS
- **Hdc2tog (half double crochet two together):** Yarn over, insert hook into next st and pull up a loop, yarn over, insert hook into next st and pull up a loop, yarn over and draw yarn through 5 loops on hook.
- **Inv dec (invisible decrease):** Insert hook into the front loop of the next 2 sts, yarn over and draw through two loops, yarn over and draw through remaining loops.
- **Popcorn:** Work 5 dc in the same st, drop loop from hook, insert hook from front to back in first dc. Put dropped loop back on hook and pull it through the st.

HEAD

Rnd 1: With **A**, 6 sc in a magic ring – 6 sts.

Rnd 2: 2 sc in each st around – 12 sts.

Rnd 3: [Sc in next st, 2 sc in next] around – 18 sts.

Rnd 4: [Sc in next 2 sts, 2 sc in next] around – 24 sts.

Rnd 5: [Sc in next 3 sts, 2 sc in next] around – 30 sts.

Rnd 6: [Sc in next 4 sts, 2 sc in next] around – 36 sts.

Rnd 7: [Sc in next 5 sts, 2 sc in next] around – 42 sts.

Rnd 8: [Sc in next 6 sts, 2 sc in next] around – 48 sts.

Rnd 9: [Sc in next 7 sts, 2 sc in next] around – 54 sts.

Rnd 10: [Sc in next 8 sts, 2 sc in next] around – 60 sts.

Rnds 11–22: Sc in each st around.

Add Safety Eyes in Rnd 18 with 10 sts between them.

Stuff the Head as you go.

Rnd 23: [Sc in next 8 sts, inv dec] around – 54 sts.

Rnd 24: [Sc in next 7 sts, inv dec] around – 48 sts.

Rnd 25: [Sc in next 6 sts, inv dec] around – 42 sts.

Rnd 26: [Sc in next 5 sts, inv dec] around – 36 sts.

Rnd 27: [Sc in next 4 sts, inv dec] around – 30 sts.

Rnd 28: [Sc in next 3 sts, inv dec] around – 24 sts.

Rnd 29: [Sc in next 2 sts, inv dec] around – 18 sts.

Rnd 30: [Sc in next st, inv dec] around – 12 sts.

Rnd 31: Inv dec around – 6 sts.

Fasten off.

HAIR

Rnd 1: With **B**, 6 sc in a magic ring – 6 sts.

Rnd 2: 2 hdc in each st around – 12 sts.

Rnd 3: [Hdc in next st, 2 hdc in next] around – 18 sts.

Rnd 4: [Hdc in next 2 sts, 2 hdc in next] around – 24 sts.

Rnd 5: [Hdc in next 3 sts, 2 hdc in next] around – 30 sts.

Rnd 6: [Hdc in next 4 sts, 2 hdc in next] around – 36 sts.

Rnd 7: [Hdc in next 5 sts, 2 hdc in next] around – 42 sts.

Rnd 8: [Hdc in next 6 sts, 2 hdc in next] around – 48 sts.

Rnds 9–14: Hdc in each st around.

Now working in rows.

Row 15: Ch 1, turn, hdc in next 21 sts.

Row 16: Ch 1, turn, sc in next 4 sts, [sc in next, (hdc, dc, hdc) in next] x3, sc in next 11 sts – 27 sts.

Fasten off, leaving a long tail for sewing.

EAR (MAKE 2)

Row 1: With **A**, 5 hdc in a magic ring – 5 sts.

Row 2: Ch 1, turn, sc in next 5 sts.

Fasten off, leaving a long tail for sewing.

MUSTACHE (MAKE 2)

Row 1: With **B**, ch 5, sc in second ch and in each ch across – 4 sts.

Row 2: Turn, sl st in second st and in each st across – 3 sts.

Fasten off, leaving a long tail for sewing.

CAPE

COLLAR

Row 1: With **D**, ch 20, hdc in second ch and in each ch across – 19 sts.

Row 2: Ch 1, turn, hdc2tog, hdc in next 15 sts, hdc2tog – 17 sts.

Row 3: Ch 1, turn, hdc in each st across.

CAPE

Join **E** with ch 1 where you ended on Row 3. First hdc-blo will be in the same st as this ch.

Row 4: Hdc-blo in each st across – 17 sts.

Row 5: Ch 1, turn, 2 hdc in next st, hdc in next 15, 2 hdc in next – 19 sts.

Row 6: Ch 1, turn, hdc in each st across.

Row 7: Ch 1, turn, 2 hdc in next st, hdc in next 17, 2 hdc in next – 21 sts.

Row 8: Ch 1, turn, hdc in each st across.

Row 9: Ch 1, turn, 2 hdc in next st, hdc in next 19, 2 hdc in next – 23 sts.

Row 10: Ch 1, turn, hdc in each st across.

Row 11: Ch 1, turn, 2 hdc in next st, hdc in next 21, 2 hdc in next – 25 sts.

Row 12: Ch 1, turn, hdc in each st across.

Row 13: Ch 1, turn, 2 hdc in next st, hdc in next 23, 2 hdc in next – 27 sts.

Row 14: Ch 1, turn, hdc in each st across.

Row 15: Ch 1, turn, 2 hdc in next st, hdc in next 25, 2 hdc in next st – 29 sts.

Row 16: Ch 1, turn, hdc in each st across.

Fasten off.

LEGS (MAKE 2)

RIGHT LEG

Rnd 1: With **C**, 6 sc in a magic ring – 6 sts.

Rnd 2: 2 sc in each st around – 12 sts.

Rnd 3: [Sc in next st, 2 sc in next] around – 18 sts.

Rnd 4: [Sc in next 2 sts, 2 sc in next] around – 24 sts.

Rnd 5: Sc-blo in each st around.

Rnd 6: Sc in each st around.

Rnd 7: Sc in next 6 sts, [inv dec] x6, sc in next 6 – 18 sts.

Rnd 8: Sc in next 6 sts, [inv dec] x3, sc in next 6 – 15 sts.

Rnds 9–11: Sc in each st around.

Rnd 12: With **D**, sc-blo in each st around.

Rnds 13–15: Sc in each st around.

Fasten off, and weave ends in. Start stuffing the Leg.

LEFT LEG

Repeat Right Leg (Rnds 1–15), but instead of cutting the yarn, join the Legs and continue with the Body.

Join the Legs.

Rnd 16: Sc in 13 on Left Leg, ch 3, join to Right Leg, 15 sc working clockwise around Right Leg – 31 sts.

Add a stitch marker at the end of this round to mark your new starting point. Do not cut yarn.

BODY

Stuff Body as you go.

Rnd 16: With **D**, [sc in next 3 chs, sc in next 15 sc] 2x – 36 sts.

Rnds 17–19: Sc in each st around.

Rnd 20: [Sc in next 16 sts, inv dec] x2 – 34 sts.

Rnd 21: Sc in each st around.

Rnd 22: [Sc in next 15 sts, inv dec] x2 – 32 sts.

Rnd 23: Sc in each st around.

Rnd 24: With **C**, [sc in next 14 sts, inv dec] x2 – 30 sts.

Rnd 25: Sc in each st around.

Rnd 26: [Sc in next 13 sts, inv dec] x2 – 28 sts.

Rnd 27: Sc in each st around.

Rnd 28: With **E**, [sc in next 12 sts, inv dec] x2 – 26 sts.

Rnd 29: Sc in each st around.

Rnd 30: [Sc in next 11 sts, inv dec] x2 – 24 sts.

Rnd 31: Sc in each st around.

Rnd 32: [Sc in next 10 sts, inv dec] x2 – 22 sts.

Rnd 33: Sc in each st around.

Fasten off, leaving a long tail for sewing.

BOOT CUFF

Join **C** in unused front loop at Leg (Rnd 12).

Rnd 1: Ch 1, sc in each st around, sl st in first st – 15 sts.

Fasten off. Repeat for second Boot Cuff.

ARMS (MAKE 2)

Rnd 1: With **A**, 5 sc in a magic ring – 5 sts.

Rnd 2: 2 sc in each st around – 10 sts.

Rnd 3: Sc in each st around.

Rnd 4: Sc in next st, popcorn in next, sc in next 8 sc – 10 sts.

Rnd 5: With **E**, sc in each st around.

Rnd 6: Sc in each st around.

Rnd 7: Sc-blo in each st around.

Rnds 8–15: Sc in each st around.

Stuff lightly, crochet across to flatten, sewing both sides together with 5 sc.

Fasten off.

SLEEVE CUFF

Join **E** in unused front loop Arm (Rnd 7) with Hand facing down.

Rnd 1: Ch 1, hdc in each st around, sl st in first st – 10 sts.

Fasten off. Repeat for second Sleeve Cuff.

ASSEMBLY

DETAILS

Embroider the Eyebrows using **F** or black thread.

With **A**, embroider the Nose, centred between the Eyes, 2–3 sts wide.

Align and pin the Hair on the Head so the fringe (puffed edge) is front facing, turned at a slight angle so it rests over one Eye, then sew in place.

Attach the Ears six sts from the outside of each Eye and in line with the Eyes.

Pin the Head onto the Body, then sew in place.

Pin the two sides of the Mustache under the Nose and sew in place.

Pin the Arms to each side of the Body, aligned with the outside of each Leg, and sew to the Neck, at Rnd 33 of Body.

Position the Cape's Collar around the back of the Neck, with edges centred over each Shoulder, and sew in place with **D**.

"THIS DEAL'S GETTING WORSE ALL THE TIME."

—Lando Calrissian, *Star Wars: Episode V–The Empire Strikes Back*

DARTH MAUL AMIGURUMI

Designed by Alexis Veenendaal

SKILL LEVEL: ✦✦✦

Darth Maul is a powerful and deadly Zabrak Sith Lord from the planet of Dathomir, where his mother served as leader of the Nightsisters. As Darth Sidious's apprentice, Darth Maul opposes the Jedi at every opportunity. In fact, it is Maul's signature, double-bladed lightsaber that ultimately brings down Jedi Master Qui-Gon Jinn. As skilled in the Force as he is with a lightsaber, this relentless Sith is not to be underestimated.

The fearsome Sith Lord makes for an almost criminally cute amigurumi in this project designed for those curious about the dark side of the Force. This pattern guides you through crocheting each part of Darth Maul individually, from his distinctive horns to his fearsome cloak. The double-bladed lightsaber is crocheted separately and can be posed in his hands for added effect. With careful colour changes and shaping, you will recreate his signature appearance stitch by stitch. Own your skills and lead with confidence as you tackle each element of this intricate design. A little of the Sith Lord's relentlessness might just come in handy for this project . . .

"AT LAST, WE WILL REVEAL OURSELVES TO THE JEDI. AT LAST, WE WILL HAVE REVENGE."

—Darth Maul, *The Phantom Menace*

SIZE
One size

FINISHED MEASUREMENTS
Height: 7 in. / 18 cm
Width: 4 in. / 10 cm

YARN
DK (4-ply) shown in Hobbii *Rainbow Cotton 8/4* (100% Cotton, 175 yd. / 160 m per 1¾ oz. / 50 g ball)
Colour A: #058 Red, 1 ball
Colour B: #009 Black, 1 ball
Colour C: #011 Dark Grey, 1 ball
Colour D: #004 Beige, 1 ball
Colour E: #016 Light Grey, 1 ball

HOOK
US C-2 / 2.5 mm crochet hook, or *size needed to obtain gauge*

NOTIONS
Pair of 8 mm black safety eyes
Tapestry needle
Locking stitch markers
Polyester stuffing
Crafting wire (optional)

GAUGE
19 sts and 24 rnds = 4 in. / 10 cm in sc
Make sure to check your gauge.

PATTERN NOTES
- The doll is worked in pieces and assembled.
- Pieces are crocheted in continuous rounds unless otherwise stated.
- The magic ring can be substituted with: Ch 2, 6 sc in second ch from hook.

SPECIAL ABBREVIATIONS
- **Inv dec (invisible decrease):** Insert hook into the front loop of the next 2 sts, yarn over and draw through two loops, yarn over and draw through remaining loops.
- **Popcorn:** Work 5 dc in the same st, drop loop from hook, insert hook from front to back in first dc. Put dropped loop back on hook and pull it through the st.

TOYS & AMIGURUMI

HEAD

Rnd 1: With **A**, 6 sc in a magic ring – 6 sts.

Rnd 2: 2 sc in each st around – 12 sts.

Rnd 3: [Sc in next st, 2 sc in next] around – 18 sts.

Rnd 4: [Sc in next 2 sts, 2 sc in next] around – 24 sts.

Rnd 5: [Sc in next 3 sts, 2 sc in next] around – 30 sts.

Rnd 6: [Sc in next 4 sts, 2 sc in next] around – 36 sts.

Now alternating between **A** and **B**.

Rnd 7: [Sc in next 5 sts, 2 sc in next] x2, sc in next 5; with **B**, 2 sc in next; with **A**, [sc in next 5, 2 sc in next] x3 – 42 sts.

Rnd 8: [Sc in next 6 sts, 2 sc in next] x2, sc in next; with **B**, sc in next; with **A**, sc in next 3; with **B**, sc in next, 2 sc in next; with **A**, sc in next 3; with **B**, sc in next; with **A**, sc in next 2, [2 sc in next, sc in next 6] x2, 2 sc in next – 48 sts.

Rnd 9: [Sc in next 7 sts, 2 sc in next] x2; with **B**, sc in next 2; with **A**, sc in next 3; with **B**, sc in next 2, 2 sc in next; with **A**, sc in next 3; with **B**, sc in next 2; with **A**, sc in next 2, [2 sc in next, sc in next 7] x2, 2 sc in next – 54 sts.

Rnd 10: [Sc in next 8 sts, 2 sc in next] x2, with **B**, sc in next 3; with **A**, sc in next 3; with **B**, sc in next 3, 2 sc in next; with **A**, sc in next 3; with **B**, sc in next 3; with **A**, sc in next, [2 sc in next, sc in next 8] x2, 2 sc in next – 60 sts.

Rnd 11: Sc in next 19 sts; with **B**, sc in next 4; with **A**, sc in next 2; with **B**, sc in next 5; with **A**, sc in next 3; with **B**, sc in next 3; with **A**, sc in next 24 – 60 sts.

Rnd 12: Sc in next 20 sts; with **B**, sc in next 2; with **A**, sc in next 4; with **B**, sc in next 4; with **A**, sc in next 4; with **B**, sc in next 2; with **A**, sc in next 24 – 60 sts.

Rnd 13: Sc in next 21 sts; with **B**, sc in next; with **A**, sc in next 5; with **B**, sc in next 2; with **A**, sc in next 6; with **B**,

sc in next; with **A**, sc in next 24 – 60 sts.

Rnd 14: Sc in next 28 sts; with **B**, sc in next; with **A**, sc in next 31 – 60 sts.

Rnd 15: Sc in each st around.

Rnd 16: Sc in next 15 sts; with **B**, sc in next 2; with **A**, sc in next 23; with **B**, sc in next 2; with **A**, sc in next 18 – 60 sts.

Rnd 17: Sc in next 16 sts; with **B**, sc in next 3; with **A**, sc in next 20; with **B**, sc in next 3; with **A**, sc in next 18 – 60 sts.

Rnd 18: Sc in next 17 sts; with **B**, sc in next 3; with **A**, sc in next 4; with **B**, sc in next; with **A**, sc in next; with **B**, sc in next; with **A**, sc in next 4; with **B**, sc in next; with **A**, sc in next; with **B**, sc in next; with **A**, sc in next 4; with **B**, sc in next 3; with **A**, sc in next 19 – 60 sts.

Rnd 19: Sc in next 18 sts; with **B**, sc in next 3; with **A**, sc in next 3; with **B**, sc in next 3; with **A**, sc in next 4; with **B**, sc in next 3; with **A**, sc in next 3; with **B**, sc in next 3; with **A**, sc in next 20 – 60 sts.

Rnd 20: Sc in next 20 sts; with **B**, sc in next 2; with **A**, sc in next 3; with **B**, sc in next 2; with **A**, sc in next 5; with **B**, sc in next 2; with **A**, sc in next 2; with **B**, sc in next 3; with **A**, sc in next 21 – 60 sts.

Rnd 21: Sc in next 21 sts; with **B**, sc in next; with **A**, sc in next 4; with **B**, sc in next; with **A**, sc in next 6; with **B**, sc in next; with **A**, sc in next 2; with **B**, sc in next; with **A**, sc in next 23 – 60 sts.

Rnd 22: Sc in next 28 sts; with **B**, sc in next; with **A**, sc in next 2; with **B**, sc in next; with **A**, sc in next 28 – 60 sts.

Add Safety Eyes in Rnd 18 with 10 sts between them.

Stuff the Head as you go.

Rnd 23: [Sc in next 8 sts, inv dec] x2, sc in next 6; with **B**, sc in next 2; with **A**, inv dec, sc in next; with **B**, sc in next 3; with **A**, sc in next 4, inv dec, [sc in next 8, inv dec] x2 – 54 sts.

Rnd 24: [Sc in next 7 sts, inv dec] x2, sc in next 6; with **B**, sc in next 3 sc; with **A**, inv dec; with **B**, sc in next 3; with **A**, sc in next 2, [inv dec, sc in next 7] x2, inv dec – 48 sts.

Rnd 25: [Sc in next 6 sts, inv dec] x2, sc in next 4, inv dec, sc in next; with **B**, sc in next 2; with **A**, sc in next 2; with **B**, sc in next 2; with **A**, sc in next, [inv dec, sc in next 6] x2, inv dec – 42 sts.

Rnd 26: [Sc in next 5 sts, inv dec] x3; with **B**, sc in next; with **A**, sc in next 2; with **B**, sc in next; with **A**, sc in next, [inv dev, sc in next 5] x2, inv dec – 36 sts.

Rnd 27: [Sc in next 4 sts, inv dec] around – 30 sts.

Rnd 28: [Sc in next 3 sts, inv dec] around – 24 sts.

Rnd 29: [Sc in next 2 sts, inv dec] around – 18 sts.

Rnd 30: [Sc in next st, inv dec] around – 12 sts.

Rnd 31: Inv dec around – 6 sts.

EAR (MAKE 2)

Row 1: With **A**, 5 hdc in a magic ring – 5 sts.

Row 2: Ch 1, turn, sc in next 5 sts.

Fasten off, leaving a long tail for sewing.

Attach the Ears 7 sts from the outside of each Eye and in line with the Eyes.

HORNS (MAKE 3)

Rnd 1: With **D**, 4 sc in a magic ring – 4 sts.

Rnd 2: Sc in each st around.

Rnd 3: [Sc in next st, 2 sc in next] x2 – 6 sts.

Rnd 4: Sc in each st around.

Rnd 5: [Sc in next st, 2 sc in next] x2 – 9 sts.

Fasten off, leaving a long tail for sewing.

LEGS (MAKE 2)

RIGHT LEG

Rnd 1: With **B**, 6 sc in a magic ring – 6 sts.

Rnd 2: 2 sc in each st around – 12 sts.

Rnd 3: [Sc in next st, 2 sc in next] around – 18 sts.

Rnd 4: [Sc in next 2 sts, 2 sc in next] around – 24 sts.

Rnd 5: Sc-blo in each st around.

Rnd 6: Sc in each st around.

Rnd 7: Sc in next 6 sts, [inv dec] x6, sc in next 6 – 18 sts.

Rnd 8: Sc in next 6 sts, [inv dec] x3, sc in next 6 – 15 sts.

Rnds 9–15: Sc in each st around.

Fasten off and weave in ends. Start stuffing the Leg.

LEFT LEG

Repeat Right Leg (Rnds 1–15) but instead of cutting the yarn, join the Legs and continue with the Body.

JOIN THE LEGS

Rnd 16: Sc in 13 sc on Right Leg, ch 3, join to Left Leg, 15 sc working clockwise around the Left Leg – 31 sts.

Add stitch marker at the end of this round to mark your new starting point. Do not cut yarn.

BODY

Stuff Body as you go.

Rnd 17: With **B**, [sc in next 3 chs, sc in next 15 sc] 2x – 36 sts.

Rnds 18–19: Sc in each st around.

Rnd 20: [Sc in next 16 sts, inv dec] x2 – 34 sts.

Rnd 21: Sc in each st around.

Rnd 22: [Sc in next 15 sts, inv dec] x2 – 32 sts.

Rnd 23: Sc in each st around.

Rnd 24: Working in blo [sc in next 14 sts, inv dec] x2 – 30 sts.

Rnd 25: Sc in each st around.

Rnd 26: With **C**, working in blo [sc in next 13 sts, inv dec] x2 – 28 sts.

Rnd 27: Sc in each st around.

Rnd 28: [Sc in next 12 sts, inv dec] x2 – 26 sts.

Rnd 29: Sc in each st around.

Rnd 30: [Sc in next 11 sts, inv dec] x2 – 24 sts.

Rnd 31: Sc in each st around.

Rnd 32: [Sc in next 10 sts, inv dec] x2 – 22 sts.

Rnd 33: Sc in each st around.

Fasten off, leaving a long tail for sewing.

TUNIC

With Head facing down, join **C** to unused front loops of Rnd 23, attaching yarn at the centre front of the Body.

Rnd 1: Ch 2, hdc in next 32 sts, sl st in first st – 32 sts.

Rnds 2–3: Ch 2, hdc in each st around, sl st in first st.

Rnd 4: Ch 2, hdc in next 8 sts, 2 hdc in next, hdc in next 16, 2 hdc in next, hdc in next 6, sl st in first st – 34 sts.

Rnd 5: Ch 2, hdc in each st around.

Now working in rows:

Rows 6–7: Ch 2, turn, hdc in each st across.

Last rnd: Ch 1, turn, sl st in next 33 sts, ch 1, work 6 sl sts into dip in the front of the tunic, sl st in first st – 39 sts.

Fasten off.

ARMS (MAKE 2)

Rnd 1: With **A**, 5 sc in a magic ring – 5 sts.

Rnd 2: 2 sc in each st around – 10 sts.

Rnd 3: Sc in each st around.

Rnd 4: Sc in next st, popcorn in next, sc in next 8 – 10 sts.

Rnd 5: Sc in each st around.

Rnds 6–15: With **C**, sc in each st around – 10 sts.

Stuff lightly, sc across to flatten, sewing both sides together with 5 sc.

Fasten off, leaving a long tail for sewing.

CLOAK

Row 1: With **B**, ch 30, sc in second ch from hook and in each ch across – 29 sts.

Row 2: Ch 1, turn, sc in next 5 sts, ch 6 (sleeve opening), skip 6, sc in next 7, ch 6 (sleeve opening), skip 6, sc in next 5 – 29 sts.

Row 3: Ch 1, turn, sc in each st across.

Rows 4–15: Ch 1, turn, hdc in each st across.

Row 16: Ch 1, turn, sc around entire Cloak, sl st in first st.

Fasten off.

SLEEVE (MAKE 2)

Join **B** in a ch around Sleeve opening (Row 2 of Cloak).

Rnd 1: Ch 1, hdc in same st, 2 hdc in next, [hdc in next, 2 hdc in next] x5 – 18 sts.

Rnds 2–6: Hdc in each st around.

Rnd 7: Hdc-blo in each st around.

Fasten off.

LIGHTSABER

Rnd 1: With **A**, 5 sc in a magic ring – 5 sts.

Rnds 2–16: Sc in each st around.

Rnds 17–21: With **E**, sc in each st around.

Rnds 22–36: With **A**, sc in each st around.

Fasten off and weave yarn through 5 sts, pull tight to close and weave in ends.

ASSEMBLY

Align and pin the Head onto the Body, then sew in place.

Pin the three Horns onto the three Black Diamonds on top of the Head and sew in place.

Pin the Arms to both sides of the Body, aligned with the outside of the Legs, and sew to the Body at Rnd 33.

DETAILS

Embroider the Eyebrows with **B** or black thread; sew the Nose centred between the Eyes, 2–3 sts wide, with **A**. Sew Lightsaber details on the Handle with **C** and **B**.

Optional: Sew the Lightsaber to Darth Maul's hand using **A**, looping it around the Handle.

Optional: Cut a straight piece of crafting wire and insert it through the centre of the Lightsaber to keep it in place.

STORMTROOPER DOLL

Designed by Leah Parker

SKILL LEVEL: / / /

An elite group of soldiers in the Imperial Army, stormtroopers are instantly recognizable for their white plastoid–plated armor, their blaster rifles, and their uniform helmets. This latter detail perhaps helped earn them the nickname "bucketheads."

In *Rogue One: A Star Wars Story*, the classic stormtrooper look is re-created in doll form—as one of many toys made by Zerpen Industries lab assistant Lyra Erso for her daughter, Jyn. Later, when Imperial death troopers capture Lyra's husband, Galen Erso, and come looking for Jyn, the stormtrooper doll is all that can be found of the young girl.

Create your own stormtrooper doll, or even an army of them, with this pattern. This slightly larger amigurumi project is crocheted from the top down, making it easy to shape the stormtrooper's signature helmet and uniform seamlessly. The arms and legs are the only elements crocheted in separate pieces. This gives them some flexibility and makes the doll more poseable—perfect for display or as a present for any young heroes-in-the-making. Just remember that, as cute as they may appear in crochet form, stormtroopers are not to be underestimated. And they don't often work alone. Then again, if you set this doll at your workstation, neither will you!

"THESE AREN'T THE DROIDS YOU'RE LOOKING FOR."

—Obi Wan Kenobi to Stormtrooper, *A New Hope*

SIZE
One size

FINISHED MEASUREMENTS
Height: 14 in. / 36 cm
Width (Head): 5 in. / 13 cm
Width (Body): 3 in. / 8 cm

YARN
Worsted weight (medium #4) shown in Lion Brand Yarn *Basic Stitch Anti-Pilling* (100% Acrylic, 185 yd. / 170 m per 3½ oz. / 100 g ball)
Colour A: #202-100 White, 1 ball
Colour B: #202-153 Black, 1 ball

HOOK
US F-5 / 3.75 mm crochet hook, or *size needed to obtain gauge*

NOTIONS
Tapestry needle
Locking stitch markers
Polyester stuffing

GAUGE
16 sts and 19 rnds = 4 in. / 10 cm in sc
Make sure to check your gauge.

PATTERN NOTES
- The doll is worked in pieces and assembled.
- Pieces are crocheted in continuous rounds unless otherwise stated.
- The magic ring can be substituted with: Ch 2, 6 sc in second ch from hook.

SPECIAL ABBREVIATION
- **4 dc bobble:** Yarn over, insert the hook into the desired stitch, *yarn over and pull up a loop. Yarn over and pull through two loops. Repeat from * three more times. Yarn over and pull through all five loops on the hook.

TOYS & AMIGURUMI

HEAD

Rnd 1: With **A**, 6 sc in a magic ring – 6 sts.

Rnd 2: 2 sc in each st around – 12 sts.

Rnd 3: [2 sc in next st, sc in next] around – 18 sts.

Rnd 4: [2 sc in next st, sc in next 2] around – 24 sts.

Rnd 5: [2 sc in next st, sc in next 3] around – 30 sts.

Rnd 6: [2 sc in next st, sc in next 4] around – 36 sts.

Rnd 7: [2 sc in next st, sc in next 5] around – 42 sts.

Rnds 8–11: Sc in each st around.

Rnds 12–13: Sc in next 10 sts; with **B**, sc in next 21 sts; with **A**, sc in next 11 sts – 42 sts.

Rnds 14–17: Sc in each st around.

Rnd 18: [4 dc bobble] in each of the next 14 sts, 14 sc, [4 dc bobble] in each of the next 14 sts, join with a sl st – 42 sts.

Rnd 19: Sc in each st around – 42 sts.

Rnd 20: [Sc in next 4 sts, sc2tog] around – 35 sts.

Rnd 21: [Sc in next 3 sts, sc2tog] around – 28 sts.

Rnd 22: [Sc in next 2 sts, sc2tog] around – 21 sts.

Stuff the Head and continue stuffing as work progresses.

HEAD DETAILS

With **B**, embroider the Eyes, Nose, and Breathing Holes.

- For the Eyes, make a triangle 5 sts long and 3 rnds high and fill it in. Embroider the Eyes 2 sts apart.
- For the Nose, work between the Eyes, one rnd down. Create an upside-down V 6 sts wide and 3 rnds high. Create a triangle below this shape that is 4 sts wide and 3 rnds deep.
- To create the Breathing Holes, embroider a small circle approximately 2 rnds by 2 sts below the Nose and to the outside edge of the Eyes.

Rnd 23: [Sc in next st, sc2tog] around – 14 sts.

Rnd 24: With **B**, sc around.

Rnd 25: 2 sc in each st around – 28 sts.

Rnd 26: [2 sc in next st, sc in next] around – 42 sts.

Rnd 27: [2 sc in next st, sc in next 2] around – 56 sts.

Rnds 28–32: With **A**, sc in each st around – 56 sts.

BODY

The next two rounds will be used to split for the Body and Arms.

Rnd 33: Sc in next 22 sts, skip 12 sts, sc in next 16. Move marker to this st, and this will be the new start of the round – 38 sts.

Rnd 34: Skip first 12 sts, sc in next 32. – 32 sts.

Rnds 35–46: Sc in each st around – 32 sts.

Stuff the Body.

BODY DETAILS

With **B**, embroider the details onto the Body:

- Make a double-thick horizontal line along Rnd 34, between the two arm openings.
- Make a double-thick vertical line between Rnds 27 and 37, centred between the armholes and going above the horizontal line.
- Make a double-thick horizontal line along Rnd 38, and another along Rnd 44.

Rnd 47: [Sc in next 2 sts, sc2tog] around – 25 sts.

Rnd 48: [Sc in next st, sc2tog] around – 16 sts.

Rnd 49: Sc2tog around – 8 sts.

Finish stuffing the Body. Fasten off and sew opening closed.

LOWER ARMS/ LOWER LEGS (MAKE 4)

Rnd 1: With **B**, 6 sc in a magic ring – 6 sts.

Rnd 2: 2 sc in each st around – 12 sts.

Rnds 3–4: Sc in each st around.

Rnds 5–12: With **A**, sc in each st around.

Fasten off and stuff.

With **B**, flatten and work 6 sc through both thicknesses across to close.

Next row: Ch 1, sc across.

Fasten off, leaving a long tail for assembly.

MID-ARM (MAKE 2)

With **A**, ch 12, sl st to close.

Rnd 1: Sc in each ch around – 12 sts.

Rnds 2–8: Sc in each st around.

Fasten off.

With **B**, flatten and work 6 sc through both thicknesses across to close bottom.

Next row: Ch 1, sc in each st across.

Fasten off, leaving a long tail for assembly.

Stuff Mid-Arm.

With **B**, flatten and work 6 sc through both thicknesses across to close top.

Next row. Ch 1, sc across.

Fasten off, leaving a long tail for assembly.

MID-LEG (MAKE 2)

With **A**, ch 12, sl st to close.

Rnd 1: Sc in each ch around – 12 sts.

Rnds 2–10: Sc in each st around.

Fasten off.

With **B**, flatten and work 6 sc through both thicknesses across to close bottom.

Next row: Ch 1, sc across.

Fasten off, leaving a long tail for assembly.

Stuff Mid-Leg.

With **B**, flatten and work 6 sc through both thicknesses across to close top.

Next row: Ch 1, sc across, turn.

Next row: Ch 1, sc across.

Fasten off, leaving a long tail for assembly.

ASSEMBLE THE ARMS

To close remaining arm openings:

With B, flatten and work 6 sc through both thicknesses across.

Row 1: Ch 1, sc across, turn.

Row 2: Ch 1, sc across.

Fasten off. Rep for second arm opening.

Sew Mid-Arm to Lower-Arm, then sew the assembled Arm to the closed arm opening. Repeat for the second Arm.

ASSEMBLE THE LEGS

Sew bottom of the Mid-Leg to Lower-Leg.

FINISHING

ASSEMBLE THE LEGS AND BODY

Sew top of Mid-Leg onto the lower Body of the Stormtrooper, level with the horizontal line on Rnd 44 of the Body. Repeat for the second Leg.

Weave in all ends.

BEHIND THE SCENES

In early drafts of the first *Star Wars* film, stormtroopers wielded their own lightsabers.

SECTION 2

COSTUMES

"I LIKE FIRSTS. GOOD OR BAD, THEY'RE ALWAYS MEMORABLE."

—Ahsoka Tano, *The Mandalorian*

First impressions make a lasting impact. And in the *Star Wars* films, the Academy Award–winning costumes are often one of the first visual insights audiences get into a character. From Han Solo to Padmé Amidala, the details of how they're dressed can reveal (or mask) key information about them. Crafted with thought and care, conceptual drawings were reportedly reviewed by George Lucas himself and stamped with "FABULOUSO" in red ink, to signal his approval.

The patterns in this section can be considered costume recreations: They're a nod to the clothes worn by the characters. Here you can learn to make a vest like Han Solo's or a wrap like Ahsoka Tano's—all made from yarn, of course. As you work your way through these projects, see if you can determine what information the costume designers were trying to convey. But remember that the finished creations are all *you*.

AHSOKA TANO'S RUANA WRAP

Designed by Leah Parker

SKILL LEVEL: ✎

Ahsoka Tano, Padawan to young Jedi Master Anakin Skywalker, is first introduced into the *Star Wars* galaxy in *The Clone Wars*. A Togruta, Ahsoka is strong, intelligent, and not afraid to speak her mind. This last trait earns her both a warning and a nickname from Anakin, when he tells her not to get "snippy" with him and begins calling her "Snips." Ahsoka is not afraid to stand up for what she believes in, and when her faith in the Jedi is shaken, she forges her own path. She continues to fight for peace while opposing the injustices of the Galactic Empire.

This ruana wrap is inspired by Ahsoka's signature cloak, which appears white after she confronts Anakin and accepts her individual journey on the light side of the Force. The speckled grey yarn used in this pattern can be a symbol of transition. A minimal number of seams makes this an approachable project for beginners, while the flowing drape of the ruana showcases the skills of seasoned crafters. The design utilizes a repeat of single and double crochets to create a beautiful silt stitch, which adds an extra dimension to the fabric. If you're new to crochet, remember to practice resilience in the face of mistakes—it is about learning and growing with each challenge, like Ahsoka does. By the end, you will have a striking, wearable piece that embodies your own journey as a crafter.

> "YOU DON'T HAVE TO CARRY A SWORD TO BE POWERFUL."
>
> —Ahsoka Tano, *The Clone Wars*

SIZE
One size

FINISHED MEASUREMENTS
Height: 70 in. / 178 cm
Width: 30 in. / 76 cm

YARN
Worsted weight (medium #4) shown in Allison Barnes Yarn *Classic Worsted* (100% Superwash Merino Wool, 200 yd. / 183 m per 115 g skein): 11 skeins in Chin Hairs.

HOOK
US J-10 / 6.00 mm crochet hook, or *size needed to obtain gauge*

NOTIONS
Tapestry needle
Locking stitch markers

GAUGE
12 sts and 7 rows = 4 in. / 10 cm in dc
Make sure to check your gauge.

PATTERN NOTES
- Back panel is crocheted first, split at the neckline into two front panels, and seamed up at the sides at finishing.
- Chains at the beginning of a row do not count as a stitch.

BACK

Row 1 (RS): Ch 111, dc in fourth ch from hook and in each ch across – 109 dc.

Row 2 (WS): Turn, ch 1, (sc, 2 dc) in first st, *skip 2 sts, (sc, 2 dc) in next st, rep from * to last three sts, skip 2 sts, sc into last st – 109 sts.

Row 3: Turn, ch 2, dc in each st across.

Rows 4–77: Rep Rows 2–3.

FRONT RIGHT

Row 78: Turn, ch 1, (sc, 2 dc) in first st, *skip 2 sts, (sc, 2 dc) in next st, rep from * 16 more times, skip 2 sts, sc in next, leave remaining sts unworked – 55 sts.

Row 79: Turn, ch 2, dc in each st across.

Rows 80–153: Rep Rows 78–79. Fasten off.

FRONT LEFT

Row 78 (continued): Join yarn in same st as last st from Front Right Panel, ch 1, (sc, 2 dc) in first st, *skip 2 sts, (sc, 2 dc) in next st, rep from * until 3 sts remain, skip 2 sts, sc in last – 55 sts.

Row 79: Turn, ch 2, dc in each st across.

Rows 80–153: Rep Rows 78-79. Fasten off.

ASSEMBLY

With RS facing each other, align the Front Right's outside edge to the Back and pin in place using locking stitch markers. Seam panels with sl sts through both thicknesses, leaving a 13 in. / 33 cm opening for the armhole. Repeat with Front Left.

FINISHING

Create a neat, finished edge around armholes and front as follows:

Join yarn to bottom of armhole.

Rnd 1: Sc evenly around, join with sl st in first sc. Fasten off.

Repeat around second armhole, and around front.

Weave in ends and block to finished measurements.

HAN SOLO'S VEST

Designed by Leah Parker

SKILL LEVEL: ///

A talented pilot known to have a reckless side, Han Solo scrapes his way from an impoverished childhood on the streets of Corellia to become the captain of the *Millennium Falcon*. Along with his co-pilot Chewbacca, Solo works as a smuggler, and the duo are often counted on to take jobs others might consider too risky. To pay off his debts to crime lord Jabba the Hutt, Solo agrees to provide passage for a Jedi and his apprentice traveling to Alderaan: Obi-Wan Kenobi and Luke Skywalker. What starts as a straightforward assignment puts Solo and Chewie on a collision course with the Imperial forces. As Solo becomes more entangled with the Rebel Alliance, he starts to believe in their cause and takes up the fight for galactic freedom.

A hero with a bit of a dark past, Han Solo is often seen wearing a dark Vest over an off-white shirt. Now his Vest can be a part of your *Star Wars* costume or used as a small nod to the galaxy in your everyday wardrobe. Just like Solo's version, this Vest has pockets that can carry a range of supplies—a key detail for a smuggler and a handy option for everyday living, too. Designed with both form and function in mind, the body of the Vest is worked in one piece from the bottom up, minimizing seams for a clean and polished finish. The pockets are crocheted separately and sewn on, adding not only visual detail but functionality.

"YOU'RE ALL CLEAR, KID. NOW LET'S BLOW THIS THING AND GO HOME."

—Han Solo, *A New Hope*

SIZES
XS (S, M, L, XL, 2X, 3X, 4X, 5X)
Instructions are written for the smallest size, with larger sizes given in parentheses; when only one number is given it applies to all sizes.

FINISHED MEASUREMENTS
Chest: 32 (36, 40, 44, 48, 52, 56, 60, 64) in. / 81 (91.5, 101.6, 111.7, 123, 132, 142, 152.4, 162.5) cm
Length: 19 (20, 21, 22, 24, 24, 25, 25, 27) in. / 48 (51, 53, 56, 61, 61, 63.5, 63.5, 68.5) cm
Armhole Depth: 9 (9, 10, 10, 11, 11, 12, 12, 13) in. / 23 (23, 25.5, 25.5, 28, 28, 30.5, 30.5, 33) cm
Sample is shown in size large.

YARN
Worsted weight (medium #4) shown in Lion Brand Yarn *Wool Ease* (80% Acrylic, 20% Wool, 197 yd. / 180 m per 3 oz. / 85 g ball): 3 (3, 4, 5, 5, 6, 6, 8) balls in #620-052 Flint.

HOOK
US J-10 / 6.00 mm, or *size needed to obtain gauge*

NOTIONS
Tapestry needle
Pins
Stitch markers

GAUGE
10 sts and 10 rows = 4 in. / 10 cm in hdc
Make sure to check your gauge.

PATTERN NOTES
- Vest is worked from bottom up in one piece.
- Pocket details are worked separately and sewn on after. Ensure that pockets are placed on the right side of the Vest.

SPECIAL ABBREVIATIONS
Hdc2tog (half double crochet two together): Yarn over, insert hook into next stitch and pull up a loop, yarn over, insert hook into next stitch and pull up a loop, yarn over and draw yarn through 5 loops on hook.

VEST

BODY

Ch 74 (84, 94, 104, 114, 124, 134, 144, 154).

Row 1 (RS): Hdc in third ch from hook and in each ch across – 72 (82, 92, 102, 112, 122, 132, 142, 152) hdc.

Row 2: Turn, ch 1, hdc in each st across.

Rows 3–25 (27, 28, 30, 32, 32, 33, 33, 35): Rep Row 2.

FRONT PANEL A

Row 26 (28, 29, 31, 33, 33, 34, 34, 36): Turn, ch 1, hdc in next 18 (21, 23, 26, 28, 31, 33, 36, 38) hdc.

Rows 27–28 (29–30, 30, 32, 34, 34, 35–36, 35–36, 37–38): Turn, ch 1, hdc in each st across.

Row 29 (31, 31, 33, 35, 35, 37, 37, 39): Turn, ch 1, hdc in each st across until 2 sts remain, hdc2tog in last 2 sts – 17 (20, 22, 25, 27, 30, 32, 35, 37) hdc.

Row 30 (32, 32, 34, 36, 36, 38, 38, 40): Turn, ch 1, hdc in each st across.

Rows 31–34 (33–40, 33–42, 35–44, 37–50, 37–52, 39–56, 39–56, 41–62): Rep previous two rows 2 (4, 5, 5, 7, 8, 9, 9, 11) times – 15 (16, 17, 20, 20, 22, 23, 26, 26) hdc remain.

Sizes XS–XL (Sizes 2X–5X to proceed to Shaping the Collar)

Rows 35–40 (41–42, 43–46, 45–48, 51–52): Turn, ch 1, hdc in each st across – 15 (16, 17, 20, 20) hdc.

SHAPING THE COLLAR

Sizes XS–2X

Row 41 (43, 47, 49, 53, 53): Turn, ch 1, hdc2tog in first 2 sts, [hdc2tog in next 2 sts] 3x, hdc in each st across – 11 (12, 13, 16, 16, 18) hdc.

Row 42 (44, 48, 50, 54, 54): Turn, ch 1, hdc in each st across.

Row 43 (45, 49, 51, 55, 55): Turn, ch 1, hdc2tog in first 2 sts, hdc2tog in next 2, hdc in each st across – 9 (10, 11, 14, 14, 16) hdc.

Row 44 (46, 50, 52, 56, 56): Turn, ch 1, hdc in each st across.

Row 45 (47, 51, 53, 57, 57): Turn, ch 1, hdc2tog in first 2 sts, hdc in each st across – 8 (9, 10, 13, 13, 15) hdc.

Rows 46–48 (48–50, 52–53, 54–55, 58–60, 58–60): Turn, ch 1, hdc in each st across.

Fasten off.

Size 3X

Row 57: Turn, ch 1, hdc2tog in first 2 sts, [hdc2tog in next 2 sts] 3x, hdc in next 13 sts, hdc2tog in last 2 – 18 hdc.

Row 58: Turn, ch 1, hdc in each st across.

Row 59: Turn, ch 1, hdc2tog in first 2 sts, hdc2tog in next 2 sts, hdc in each st across – 16 hdc.

Row 60: Turn, ch 1, hdc in each st across.

Row 61: Turn, ch 1, hdc2tog in first 2 sts, hdc in each st across – 15 hdc.

Rows 62–63: Turn, ch 1, hdc in each st across.

Fasten off.

Sizes 4X–5X

Row 57 (63): Turn, ch 1, hdc2tog in first 2 sts, [hdc2tog in next 2 sts] 3x, hdc in next 16 sts, hdc2tog in last 2 – 21 hdc.

Row 58 (64): Turn, ch 1, hdc in each st across.

Row 59 (65): Turn, ch 1, hdc2tog in first 2 sts, hdc2tog in next 2 sts, hdc

in next 15, hdc2tog in last 2 – 18 hdc.

Row 60 (66): Turn, ch 1, hdc in each st across.

Row 61 (67): Turn, ch 1, hdc2tog in first 2 sts, hdc in each st across – 17 hdc.

Row(s) 62–63 (68): Turn, ch 1, hdc in each st across.

Fasten off.

BACK PANEL

Attach yarn in unworked stitch after Front Panel A.

Row 26 (28, 29, 31, 33, 33, 34, 34, 36): Turn, ch 1, hdc in next 36 (40, 46, 50, 56, 60, 66, 70, 76) sts.

Rows 27–28 (29–30, 30, 32, 34, 34, 35–36, 35–36, 37–38): Turn, ch 1, hdc across.

Row 29 (31, 31, 33, 35, 35, 37, 37, 39): Turn, ch 1, hdc2tog in first 2 sts, hdc across until 2 sts remain, hdc2tog in last 2 – 34 (38, 44, 48, 54, 58, 64, 68, 74) hdc.

Row 30 (32, 32, 34, 36, 36, 38, 38, 40): Turn, ch 1, hdc in each st across.

Rows 31–34 (33–40, 33–42, 35–44, 37–50, 37–52, 39–58, 39–60, 41–66): Rep previous two rows 2 (4, 5, 5, 7, 8, 10, 11, 13) times – 30 (30, 34, 38, 40, 42, 44, 46, 48) hdc remain.

Sizes XS–4X (Size 5X continue to next section)

Row(s) 35–46 (41–48, 43–51, 45–53, 51–58, 53–58, 59–61, 61): Turn, ch 1, hdc in each st across.

All sizes

Rows 47–48 (49–50, 52–53, 54–55, 59–60, 59–60, 62–63, 62–63, 67–68): Turn, ch 1, hdc in next 8 (9, 10, 13, 13, 15, 15, 17, 17) sts, sc in next 14 (12, 14, 12, 14, 12, 14, 12, 14), hdc in next 8 (9, 10, 13, 13, 15, 15, 17, 17).

Fasten off.

FRONT PANEL B

Attach yarn in unworked stitch after Back Panel.

Row 26 (28, 29, 31, 33, 33, 34, 34, 36): Turn, ch 1, hdc in next 18 (21, 23, 26, 28, 31, 33, 36, 38) sts.

Rows 27–28 (29–30, 30, 32, 34, 34, 35–36, 35–36, 37–38): Turn, ch 1, hdc across.

Row 29 (31, 31, 33, 35, 35, 37, 37, 39): Turn, ch 1, hdc2tog in first 2 sts, hdc in each st across – 17 (20, 22, 25, 27, 30, 32, 35, 37) hdc.

Row 30 (32, 32, 34, 36, 36, 38, 38, 40): Turn, ch 1, hdc in each st across.

Rows 31–34 (33–40, 33–42, 35–44, 37–50, 37–52, 39–56, 39–56, 41–62): Rep previous two rows 2 (4, 5, 5, 7, 8, 9, 9, 11) times – 15 (16, 17, 20, 20, 22, 23, 26, 26) hdc remain.

Sizes XS–XL (Sizes 2X–5X to proceed to Shaping the Collar)

Rows 35–40 (41–42, 43–46, 45–48, 51–52): Turn, ch 1, hdc in each st across.

SHAPING THE COLLAR
Sizes XS–2X

Row 41 (43, 47, 49, 53, 53): Turn, ch 1, hdc in next 7 (8, 9, 12, 12) sts, [hdc2tog in next 2 sts] 4x – 11 (12, 13, 16, 16, 18) hdc.

Row 42 (44, 48, 50, 54, 54): Turn, ch 1, hdc in each st across.

Row 43 (45, 49, 51, 55, 55): Turn, ch 1, hdc in next 7 (8, 9, 12, 12) sts, [hdc2tog in next 2 sts] twice – 9 (10, 11, 14, 14, 16) hdc.

Row 44 (46, 50, 52, 56, 56): Turn, ch 1, hdc in each st across.

Row 45 (47, 51, 53, 57, 57): Turn, ch 1, hdc in next 7 (8, 9, 12, 12) sts, hdc2tog in last 2 sts – 8 (9, 10, 13, 13, 15) hdc.

Rows 46–48 (48–50, 52–53, 54–55, 58–60, 58–60): Turn, ch 1, hdc in each st across.

Fasten off.

Size 3X

Row 57: Turn, ch 1, hdc2tog in first 2 sts, hdc in next 13 sts, [hdc2tog in next 2 sts] 4x – 18 hdc.

Row 58: Turn, ch 1, hdc in each st across.

Row 59: Turn, ch 1, hdc in each st across until 4 sts remain, [hdc2tog in next 2 sts] twice – 16 hdc.

Row 60: Turn, ch 1, hdc in each st across.

Row 61: Turn, ch 1, hdc in each st across until 2 sts remain, hdc2tog in last 2 sts – 15 hdc.

Rows 62–63: Turn, ch 1, hdc in each st across.

Fasten off.

Sizes 4X–5X

Row 57 (63): Turn, ch 1, hdc2tog in first 2 sts, hdc in next 16, [hdc2tog in next 2 sts] 4x – 21 hdc.

Row 58 (64): Turn, ch 1, hdc in each st across.

Row 59 (65): Turn, ch 1, hdc2tog in first 2 sts, hdc in each st across until 4 sts remain, [hdc2tog in next 2 sts] twice – 18 hdc.

Row 60 (66): Turn, ch 1, hdc in each st across.

Row 61 (67): Turn, ch 1, hdc in each st across until 2 sts remain, hdc2tog in last 2–17 hdc.

Row(s) 62–63 (68): Turn, ch 1, hdc in each st across.

Fasten off.

POCKET DETAILS

UPPER BACK POCKET (MAKE 4 – 1 TO 4 ON SCHEMATIC)

Ch 7 (7, 8, 9, 9, 10, 10, 11, 11).

Row 1 (RS): Hdc in third ch from hook and in each ch across – 5 (5, 6, 7, 7, 8, 8, 9, 9) hdc.

Row 2: Turn, ch 1, hdc in each st across.

Rows 3–16: Rep Row 2.

Fasten off leaving a 12 in. / 30 cm tail for sewing onto Vest.

LOWER BACK POCKET (5 ON SCHEMATIC)

Part A—Pocket

Ch 27 (27, 30, 34, 37, 38, 40, 42, 44).

Row 1 (RS): Hdc in third ch from hook and in hdc in each ch across – 25 (25, 28, 32, 35, 36, 38, 40, 42) hdc.

Row 2: Turn, ch 1, hdc in each st across.

Rows 3–18 (19, 20, 20, 22, 22, 23, 23, 23): Rep Row 2.

Fasten off leaving a 24 in. / 61 cm tail for sewing onto Vest.

Part B—Flap

Ch 27 (27, 30, 34, 37, 38, 40, 42, 44)

Row 1 (RS): Hdc in third ch from hook and in each ch across – 25 (25, 28, 32, 35, 36, 38, 40, 42) hdc.

Row 2: Turn, ch 1, hdc in each st across.

Rows 3–4 (4, 6, 6, 6, 6, 8, 8, 8, 8): Rep Row 2.

Fasten off leaving a 12 in. / 30 cm tail for sewing onto Vest.

LOWER FRONT POCKET (MAKE 2 – 6 AND 7 ON SCHEMATIC)

Part A—Pocket

Ch 10 (13, 15, 18, 20, 23, 25, 28, 30).

Row 1 (RS): Hdc in third ch from hook and in each ch across – 8 (11, 13, 16, 18, 21, 23, 26, 28) hdc.

Row 2: Turn, ch 1, hdc in each st across.

Rows 3–12 (13, 14, 14, 15, 15, 17, 17, 17): Rep Row 2.

Fasten off leaving a 12 in. / 30 cm tail for sewing onto Vest.

Part B—Flap

Ch 10 (13, 15, 18, 20, 23, 25, 28, 30).

Row 1 (RS): Hdc in third ch from hook and in each ch across – 8 (11, 13, 16, 18, 21, 23, 26, 28) hdc.

Row 2: Turn, ch 1, hdc in each st across.

Rows 3–4 (4, 6, 6, 6, 6, 8, 8, 8): Rep Row 2.

Fasten off leaving a 12 in. / 30 cm tail for sewing onto Vest.

UPPER FRONT POCKET (MAKE 2 – 8 AND 9 ON SCHEMATIC)

Part A—Pocket

Ch 11 (12, 14, 16, 16, 19, 19, 20, 20).

Row 1 (RS): Hdc in third ch from hook and in each ch across – 9 (10, 12, 14, 14, 17, 17, 18, 18) hdc.

Row 2: Turn, ch 1, hdc in each st across.

Rows 3–12 (13, 14, 14, 15, 15, 17, 17, 17): Rep Row 2.

Fasten off leaving a 12 in. / 30 cm tail for sewing onto Vest.

Part B—Flap

Ch 11 (12, 14, 16, 16, 19, 19, 20, 20)

Row 1 (RS): Hdc in third ch from hook and in each ch across – 9 (10, 12, 14, 14, 17, 17, 18, 18) hdc.

Row 2: Turn, ch 1, hdc in each st across.

Rows 3–4 (4, 6, 6, 6, 6, 8, 8, 8): Rep Row 2.

Fasten off leaving a 12 in. / 30 cm tail for sewing onto Vest.

FINISHING AND ASSEMBLY

- Block Vest and Pocket details to finished measurements.

BACK PANEL

- Place bottom of Pocket 1 on Row 26 (28, 29, 31, 33, 33, 34, 34, 36), with the top left corner approximately 1 in. / 2.5 cm in from the narrowest portion of the Back Panel. Pin in place.
- Place Pocket 4 at opposite end of same row and aligned with Pocket 1. Pin in place.
- Evenly space Pockets 2 and 3 between Pockets 1 and 4. Pin in place.
- Place the bottom of Pocket 5A on Row 4 and in line with the outer edges of Pockets 1 and 4. Pin in place.
- Place Pocket 5B two rows above and in line with the outer edges of Pocket 5A. Pin in place.

FRONT PANELS

- Place the bottom of Pocket 6A on Row 4, approximately 1 in. / 2.5 cm from the outside bottom edge of the Front Panel. Pin in place.
- Place Pocket 6B two rows above and in line with the outer edges of Pocket 6A. Pin in place.
- Repeat with Pockets 7A and 7B on second Front Panel.
- Place the bottom of Pocket 8A on Row 26 (28, 29, 31, 33, 33, 34, 34, 36), approximately 1 in. / 2.5 cm from the outside edge of the Panel. Pin in place.
- Place Pocket 8B two rows above and in line with the outer edges of Pocket 8A. Pin in place.
- Repeat with Pockets 9A and 9B on second Front Panel.
- Once all Pockets are pinned onto the Vest and you have confirmed their placement, sew them in place.
- Pockets 1, 2, 3, 4, 5A, 6A, 7A, 8A, 9A: Sew along right side, bottom and left side, leaving the top open.
- Pockets 5B, 6B, 7B, 8B, 9B: Sew only along the top.
- Seam the Shoulders of the Front Panels onto the Back Panel.
- Attach yarn to the bottom of the armhole and evenly sc around for two rounds. Fasten off. Repeat on other side.
- Join yarn to the bottom of the Vest and evenly sc around (at Row 29 (31, 31, 33, 35, 35, 37, 37, 39) on the Front Panels, make 4 sc). Work another round of sc. Fasten off.
- Weave in ends.

SCHEMATIC

FRONT

3 (3.5, 4, 5, 5, 6, 6, 6.5, 6.5)"
7.5, (9, 10, 13, 13, 15, 15, 16.5, 16.5) cm

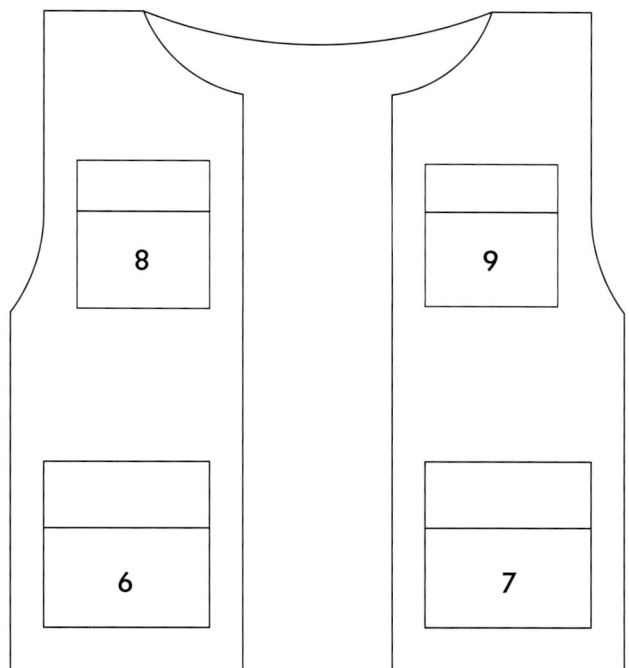

9 (9, 10, 10, 11, 11, 12, 12, 13)"
23 (23, 25.5, 25.5, 28, 28, 30.5, 30.5, 33) cm

19 (20, 21, 22, 24, 24, 25, 25, 27)"
48 (51, 53, 56, 61, 61, 63.5, 63.5, 68.5) cm

10 (11, 11, 12, 13, 13, 13, 13, 14)"
25.5 (28, 28, 30.5, 33, 33, 33, 33, 35.5) cm

7 (8, 25, 9, 10.25, 11, 12.25, 13, 14.25, 15)"
18 (21, 23, 26, 28, 31, 33, 36, 38) cm

28.5 (32.5, 36.5, 40.5, 44.5, 48.5, 52.5, 56.5, 60.5)"
72.5 (82.5, 93, 103, 113, 123, 133.5, 143.5, 154) cm

BACK

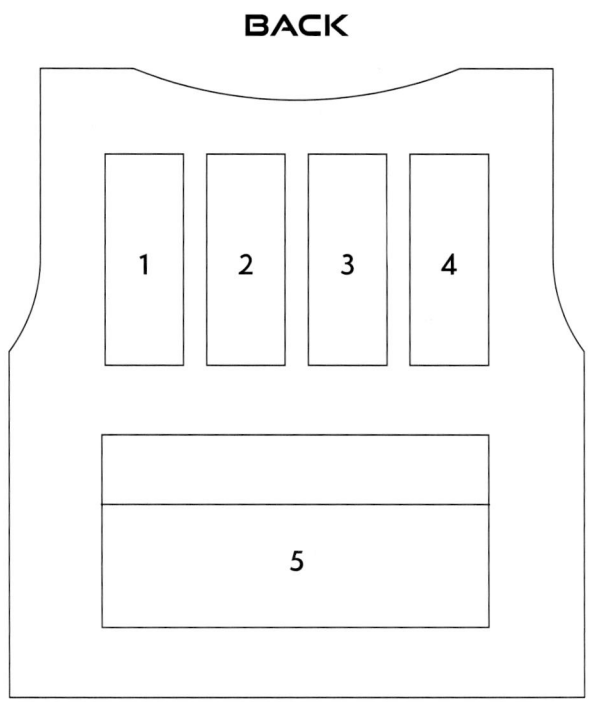

"NEVER TELL ME THE ODDS."

—Han Solo, *The Empire Strikes Back*

COSTUMES 61

PHANTOM MENACE SCARF

Designed by Leah Parker

SKILL LEVEL: ///

When a dispute between the Trade Federation and the outlying system of the Galactic Republic leads to a blockade of the planet Naboo, Jedi Master Qui-Gon Jinn and his Padawan Obi-Wan Kenobi arrive on the scene as ambassadors. They manage to rescue Naboo's queen, Amidala, planning to escort her to Coruscant so that she can issue a formal request for help from the Galactic Senate. This journey puts the queen and the Jedi on a path to meet Anakin Skywalker, an enslaved child working in a junk shop. Anakin grows close with Qui-Gon Jinn and Obi-Wan Kenobi. The Jedi sense his strong connection to the Force, though it's not immediately clear to them whether he will bring balance or tip the scales to the light or dark side. Meanwhile, Amidala makes an indelible mark of her own on Anakin, and he never forgets their first meeting.

Inspired by the blanket that Padmé gives Anakin to keep warm aboard the Naboo Royal Starship, this scarf will help keep you cosy during your own adventures. Its design utilizes simple yet striking colourwork techniques to re-create the look and feel of the blanket. As you work your way through this one, keep in mind that Padmé's blanket represents a gesture of kindness at an uncertain time. No matter who or what you intend this scarf for, crochet it with that same spirit and you can't go wrong.

"YOU COME FROM A WARM PLANET, ANI.
A LITTLE TOO WARM FOR MY TASTE."

—Padmé Amidala, *The Phantom Menace*

SIZE
One size

FINISHED MEASUREMENTS
Length: 65 in. / 158 cm
Width: 9 in. / 23 cm

YARN
Worsted weight (medium #4) shown in Madelinetosh *Tosh Vintage* (100% Superwash Merino Wool, 200 yd. / 182 m per 114 g skein)
Colour A: Blood Runs Cold, 3 skeins
Colour B: Paper, 1 skein

HOOK
US H-8 / 5.00 mm crochet hook, or *size needed to obtain gauge*

NOTIONS
Tapestry needle
Locking stitch markers

GAUGE
15 sts and 12 rows = 4 in. / 10 cm in hdc
Make sure to check your gauge.

PATTERN NOTES
- When working in front of the previous row, keep the chain spaces of the current row to the back of the project and work in the indicated stitch one or more rows below.
- When colour is not in use, fasten off and reattach when needed again.

PATTERN

Row 1: With **A**, ch 34, sc in second ch from hook and in each ch across – 33 sts.

Row 2 (WS): Turn, ch 1, sc in next 3 sts, *ch 1, skip next st, sc in next st, ch 1, skip next st, sc in next 3 sts, rep from * across.

Row 3 (RS): Tzzurn, ch 1, sc in next 3 sts, *working in front of previous row, dc in next st 2 rows below, ch 1, skip next st, working in front of previous row, dc in next st 2 rows below**, ch 3, skip next 3 sts, rep from * across, ending last rep at **, sc in last 3 sts.

Row 4: Turn, ch 1, sc in next 3 sts, *ch 3, skip next 3 sts**, working in front of the previous row, dc in next 3 sts two rows below, rep from * across, ending last rep at **, sc in last 3 sts. Fasten off.

Row 5: Join **B**, turn, ch 1, sc in next 3 sts, *working in front of the previous row, dc in next st 2 rows below, tr in next st 3 rows below, dc in next st 2 rows below, sc in next 3 dc, rep from * across.

Rows 6–8: Rep Rows 2–4.
Row 9: With **A**, rep Row 5.
Rows 10–12: Rep Rows 2–4.
Row 13: With **B**, rep Row 5.
Rows 14–16: Rep Rows 2–4.
Row 17: With **A**, rep Row 5.
Row 18: Turn, ch 1, *sc in next 3 sts, hdc in next 3 sts, rep from * across, sc in last 3 sts.
Rows 19–167: Turn, ch 1, hdc in each st across.
Rows 168–170: Rep Rows 2–4.
Row 171: With **B**, rep Row 5.
Rows 172–174: Rep Rows 2–4.
Row 175: With **A**, rep Row 5.
Rows 176–178: Rep Rows 2–4.
Row 179: With **B**, rep Row 5.
Rows 180-182: Rep Rows 2–4.
Row 183: With **A**, rep Row 5.
Row 184: Turn, ch 1, *sc in next 3 sts, hdc in next 3 sts, rep from * across, sc in last 3 sts.
Row 185: Turn, ch 1, hdc in each st across.

Fasten off and weave in all ends.

Block scarf to finished measurements.

JYN ERSO'S HOODED COWL

Designed by Kate Hammitt

SKILL LEVEL: ✦✦✦

Rogue One, a stand-alone film in the *Star Wars* galaxy, follows a group of unlikely heroes who join together on a mission to steal the Galactic Empire's schematics for the space station known as the Death Star. These plans are held in a vault in the Imperial Centre of Military Research on the planet Scarif. A heavily guarded location, the Rebel Alliance considers any possible heist highly dangerous. However, Jyn Erso, the daughter of the Death Star's reluctant engineer, is determined to gain access to her father's designs on behalf of the Alliance. Nicknamed Stardust by her family, Jyn is bright, brave, and independent. Using intel her father has shared via holographic recording, she leads a group of volunteers on an unauthorized quest that will change the course of the war. Bodhi Rook gives them the call sign Rogue One

Inspired by the cowl Jyn wears in the film, this hooded, shoulder-length cloak may be just what your next mission calls for. Whether you're among trusted allies or in need of a little discretion, pull on this cowl and know that you're covered. Like many plans, this pattern requires multiple steps. Fortunately, it uses the sieve stitch, which is resilient and adaptable, much like Jyn. The cowl itself is worked in the round, allowing for a seamless construction that easily fits to your measurements. Once the cowl is complete, the hood is shaped back and forth in rows.

"REBELLIONS ARE BUILT ON HOPE."

—Jyn Erso, *Rogue One: A Star Wars Story*

SIZE
One size

FINISHED MEASUREMENTS
COWL
Height: 8 in. / 20 cm
Circumference: 26 in. / 66 cm
HOOD
Length: 7 in. / 18 cm
Width: 13 in. / 33 cm

YARN
Fingering weight (superfine #1) shown in Mace of Skeins *Spade* (85% Superwash Merino, 15% Nylon, 437 yd. / 399 m per 100 g skein): 2 skeins in Rogue.

HOOK
US F-5 / 3.75 mm crochet hook, or *size needed to obtain gauge*

NOTIONS
Tapestry needle
Locking stitch markers

GAUGE
26 sts and 27 rows = 4 in. / 10 cm in pattern, blocked
Make sure to check your gauge.

PATTERN NOTES
- Crocheted using the sieve stitch, this is a beginner-friendly pattern featuring a reversible fabric.
- Cowl is worked in turned rounds; hood is worked in rows.

SPECIAL ABBREVIATIONS
- **Fsc (foundation single crochet):** Begin with a slip knot on your hook and chain two. Insert hook into the first chain, *yarn over and pull up a loop, yarn over and pull through one loop on hook (chain made), yarn over and pull through remaining loops on hook (sc made). Insert hook in chain just made and repeat from * until you have made the required number of stitches.

COSTUMES

COWL

Rnd 1: Fsc 156, sl st in first fsc to join – 156 sts.

Rnd 2: Ch 1, turn, sc in first st, *ch 1, sk next**, sc in next, rep from * around, ending last rep at ** sl st in first st to join – 156 sts.

Rnd 3: Ch 1, turn, *2 sc in ch sp, sk next sc, rep from * around, sl st in first st to join.

Rnds 4–55: Rep Rnds 2–3 until Cowl measures 8 in. / 20 cm or desired length is reached.

HOOD

Row 1: Ch 1, turn, sc-flo in first st, [ch 1, sk next, sc-flo in next] 3x, *ch 1, sk next, sc in next, rep from * around. Now working in unused loops of initial 8 sts, [sc-blo in next**, ch 1, sk next] 4x, ending last repeat at ** – 163 sts.

Row 2: Ch 1, turn, sc in first st, *ch 1, sk next, sc in next, rep from * across.

Row 3: Ch 1, turn, *2 sc in ch sp, sk next sc, rep from * to last st, sc in last st.

Rows 4–51: Rep Rows 2–3 until Hood measures 7 in. / 18 cm or until desired length is reached. End with a repeat of Row 2.

HOOD SHAPING

Row 1: Ch 1, turn, 2 sc in each ch sp until 110 sts have been made.

Row 2: Turn, sc in first st, *ch 1, sk next, sc in next, rep until 57 sts have been made.

Work across these sts, joining work to either side of the Hood as you go:

Row 3: Turn, 2 sc in each ch sp to last sc, sc2tog (with the last st and next unworked st from Row 1), sc in next – 58 sts.

Row 4: Turn, skip first sc, sc in next st, *ch 1, sk next, sc in next, rep from * to end, sl st twice on Hood – 57 sts.

Row 5: Turn, sk both sl sts, 2 sc in each ch sp to last sc, sc2tog (with the last st and next unworked st from Row 1) – 58 sts.

Rows 6–55: Rep Rows 4–5 until all sts on Hood have been worked.

Fasten off.

HOOD EDGING

With RS facing, join yarn to bottom right edge of Hood, where it meets the Cowl.

Row 1: Sc in each row end and st across to left edge of Hood.

Fasten off and weave in ends.

FINISHING

Wet block. Lay flat to dry.

PADMÉ AMIDALA'S BATTLE WRAP

Designed by Kate Hammitt

SKILL LEVEL: ✦

Padmé Amidala, first queen and later senator of Naboo, is a courageous politician dedicated to protecting peace in the galaxy. First elected to the role of queen at the age of fourteen, Amidala grew up in the public eye, immersed in politics. As queen, Amidala refuses to sign a treaty with the Trade Federation that would legitimize their occupation of her home planet—despite the risk this stance poses to her own safety.

When her position calls for it, Amidala can be seen dressed in elaborate outfits made of silk, lace, and delicate embroidery. But when practicality requires it, she appears in clothes more adaptable to the landscape. For example, she dons a battle wrap to rescue her old friend Obi-Wan Kenobi when he's in need. This pattern re-creates Amidala's wrap as a "shlanket." Part shawl, part blanket—it's nearly as adaptable as its on-screen inspiration. This project may technically fall somewhere between a costume and inspired clothing, but that ambiguity seems *just right* for a queen known to dress in disguise.

> "HE GAVE YOU STRICT ORDERS TO PROTECT ME, AND I'M GOING TO HELP OBI-WAN. IF YOU PLAN TO PROTECT ME, YOU'LL JUST HAVE TO COME ALONG."
>
> —Padmé Amidala, *Attack of the Clones*

SIZE
One size

FINISHED MEASUREMENTS
Length: 45 in. / 114.5 cm
Length (Strips): 36 in. / 91.5 cm
Width: 32 in. / 81 cm

YARN
Sport weight (fine #2) shown in Go Handmade *Curly* (59% Polyester, 12% Nylon, 29% Acrylic, 131 yd. / 120 m per 50 g ball): 13 balls in #17640 Beige.

HOOK
G-6 / 4.00 mm crochet hook, or *size needed to obtain gauge*

NOTIONS
Tapestry needle
Locking stitch markers

GAUGE
15 sts and 13 rows = 4 in. / 10 cm in hdc
Make sure to check your gauge.

PATTERN NOTES
- Pattern is worked back and forth, in rows.
- Customize the length by adding or subtracting 5 stitches for every 1 in. / 2.5 cm change.
- Customize the width by adding or subtracting 4 stitches for every 1 in. / 2.5 cm change, making sure to maintain an even number of stitches.

SPECIAL ABBREVIATIONS
- **Fhdc (foundation half double crochet):** Begin with a slip knot on your hook and chain two. Yarn over, insert hook into second chain from hook, *yarn over and pull up a loop, yarn over and pull through first loop on hook (chain made), yarn over and pull through remaining loops (hdc made). Yarn over, insert hook into last chain made and repeat from * until you have made the required number of stitches.
- **Hdc2tog (half double crochet two together):** Yarn over, insert hook into next stitch and pull up a loop, yarn over, insert hook into next stitch and pull up a loop, yarn over and draw yarn through 5 loops on hook.

COSTUMES 71

BODY

Row 1: Fhdc 120, turn.

Row 2: Ch 1, hdc in each st across, turn – 120 sts.

Rows 3–146: Rep Row 2 until fabric measures 42 in. / 108 cm or desired length.

Do not fasten off. Continue to First Strip.

FIRST STRIP

Row 1: Ch 1, hdc in next 60 sts, turn.

Rows 2–9: Rep Row 1 – 60 sts.

Row 10: Ch 1, hdc in each st across until 2 sts remain, hdc2tog, turn – 59 sts.

Row 11: Ch 1, hdc2tog, hdc in each st across, turn – 58 sts.

Rows 12–44: Rep Rows 10–11 – 25 sts remain.

Row 45: Ch 1, hdc in next 25 sts, turn.

Rows 46–92: Rep Row 45 until fabric measures 14 in. / 61 cm from last decrease (Row 44), or until desired length – 25 sts.

Row 93: Ch 1, hdc2tog, hdc in each st across, turn – 24 sts.

Row 94: Ch 1, hdc in each st across until 2 sts remain, hdc2tog, turn – 23 sts.

Rows 95–116: Rep Rows 93–94 – 1 st remains.

Fasten off and weave in ends.

SECOND STRIP

Row 1: Join in first unworked st of Row 146 of Body, ch 1, hdc in next 60 sts.

Rows 2–9: Ch 1, hdc in each st across – 60 sts.

Row 10: Ch 1, hdc2tog, hdc in each st across, turn – 59 sts.

Row 11: Ch 1, hdc in each st across until 2 sts remain, hdc2tog, turn – 58 sts.

Rows 12–44: Rep Rows 10–11 – 25 sts remain.

Row 45: Ch 1, hdc in next 25 sts, turn.

Rows 46–92: Rep Row 45 until fabric measures 14 in. / 61 cm from last decrease (Row 44), or until desired length, matching First Strip – 25 sts.

Row 93: Ch 1, hdc in each st across until 2 sts remain, hdc2tog, turn – 24 sts.

Row 94: Ch 1, hdc2tog, hdc in each st across, turn – 23 sts.

Rows 95–116: Rep Rows 93–94 – 1 st remains.

Fasten off and weave in ends.

Block to finished measurements.

ANAKIN SKYWALKER:
"YOU CALL THIS A DIPLOMATIC SOLUTION?"

PADMÉ AMIDALA:
"NO. I CALL IT AGGRESSIVE NEGOTIATIONS."

—*Star Wars: Episode II— Attack of the Clones*

SECTION 3

INSPIRED CLOTHING

QUI-GON JINN:
"AND YOU'RE SURE THERE'S NOTHING LEFT ON BOARD?"

OBI-WAN KENOBI:
"A FEW CONTAINERS OF SUPPLIES. THE QUEEN'S WARDROBE, MAYBE, BUT . . . NOT ENOUGH FOR YOU TO BARTER WITH. NOT IN THE AMOUNTS YOU'RE TALKING ABOUT."

—*The Phantom Menace*

As their dialogue in *The Phantom Menace* suggests, Jedi Master Qui-Gon Jinn and his Padawan Obi-Wan Kenobi consider Queen Amidala's clothes when looking for resources to trade or sell. Queen Amidala is similarly practical with her wardrobe, using her expected royal attire to disguise herself and a body double. In that same spirit, the projects in this section are all about bringing *Star Wars* visuals into your day-to-day look. You'll find elegant patterns, like a jumper inspired by Amidala's handmaidens, and cosy comforts, like a tauntaun-inspired cowl bound to keep you warm, even on the icy planet of Hoth. For the young Padawans in your life, there are adorable projects ranging from an Ewok-inspired toque to a Grogu bonnet. In the end, you'll have a range of gorgeous pieces fit for royalty.

AKI-AKI FESTIVAL OF THE ANCESTORS SHAWL

Designed by Leah Parker

SKILL LEVEL: ✎

Hundreds of thousands of visitors come to enjoy dancing, singing, food, and kite flying during the Aki-Aki Festival of the Ancestors on the desert planet Pasaana. This vibrant celebration is considered an opportunity to honour the past as well as to look to the future. The festival, held every forty-two years, is a cherished tradition for the Aki-Aki. Attendees include Aki-Aki spiritual leaders as well as visitors from offworld drawn to the event's joyful atmosphere. The Aki-Aki value hospitality and often welcome their guests with gifts and stories to make them feel at home, regardless of where they come from.

Bring home your own colourful souvenir in the form of this shawl, which draws inspiration from the iconic kites flown at the Festival of the Ancestors. It's designed with that same playful adaptability in mind and can be draped loosely around your shoulders or wrapped in a fitted approach to suit your style. Crocheted from the top down, the steady and consistent increases in each row may start to feel like their own rhythm, so you can ride the waves as you move from one yarn colour to the next, like a kite floating in the breeze.

POE DAMERON: "WHAT IS THIS?"
C-3PO: "THE AKI-AKI FESTIVAL OF THE ANCESTORS. THE CELEBRATION OCCURS ONCE EVERY FORTY-TWO YEARS."
FINN: "WELL, THAT'S LUCKY."
C-3PO: "LUCKY INDEED. THIS FESTIVAL IS KNOWN FOR BOTH ITS COLOURFUL KITES AND ITS DELECTABLE SWEETS."

—*Star Wars: Episode IX—The Rise of Skywalker*

SIZE
One size

FINISHED MEASUREMENTS
Height: 35 in. / 89 cm
Width: 76 in. / 193 cm

YARN
Worsted weight (medium #4) shown in Madelinetosh *Tosh Vintage* (100% Superwash Merino Wool, 200 yd. / 182 m per 114 g skein)
Colour A: Candlewick, 2 skeins
Colour B: Jaded Dreams, 3 skeins
Colour C: Horn, 2 skeins

HOOK
US H-8 / 5.00 mm crochet hook, or *size needed to obtain gauge*

NOTIONS
Tapestry needle
Locking stitch markers

GAUGE
13 sts and 12 rows = 4 in. / 10 cm in hdc
Make sure to check your gauge.

PATTERN NOTES
- Crocheted from the top down with four increases per row, this wrap works up quickly.
- Ch 3 at the beginning of a row counts as first hdc and ch 1.
- At colour changes, fasten off working yarn and join new colour.
- In addition to the hdc, each row has a ch-1 space at either end, and a ch-2 space in the centre. These are excluded from st counts for clarity.

INSPIRED CLOTHING

PATTERN

Row 1: With **A** and starting in a magic ring, ch 3, hdc, ch 2, hdc, ch 1, hdc – 4 hdc.

Row 2: Turn, ch 3, hdc in first ch sp, hdc in next st, (hdc, ch 2, hdc) in ch-2 sp, hdc in next, (hdc, ch 1, hdc) in last ch sp – 8 hdc.

Row 3: Turn, ch 3, hdc in first ch sp, hdc in each st to ch-2 sp, (hdc, ch 2, hdc) in ch-2 sp, hdc in each st to last ch sp, (hdc, ch 1, hdc) in last ch sp – 12 hdc.

Rows 4–10: Rep Row 3 – 40 hdc.

Rows 11–30: With **B**, rep Row 3 – 120 hdc.

Rows 31–32: With **A**, rep Row 3 – 128 hdc.

Rows 33–48: With **B**, rep Row 3 – 192 hdc.

Rows 49–50: With **C**, rep Row 3 – 200 hdc.

Rows 51–52: With **B**, rep Row 3 – 208 hdc.

Rows 53–54: With **A**, rep Row 3 – 216 hdc.

Rows 55–64: With **C**, rep Row 3 – 256 hdc.

Rows 65–66: With **B**, rep Row 3 – 264 hdc.

Rows 67–68: With **C**, rep Row 3 – 272 hdc.

Rows 69–76: With **A**, rep Row 3 – 304 hdc.

Rows 77–78: With **B**, rep Row 3 – 312 hdc.

TAUNTAUN COWL

Designed by Janine Mudge

SKILL LEVEL: ✎ ✎ ✎

When members of the Rebel Alliance need to traverse the snowy surface of the planet Hoth, they can't always rely on snowspeeders. The planet's extreme weather makes them unreliable. So, when Luke Skywalker is injured during a patrol mission on Hoth, Han Solo rides out to find him on the back of a giant snow lizard known as a tauntaun. With their large hind legs, fierce-looking horns, and resilience against the cold, these creatures are well suited to surviving on Hoth. That is, barring any run-ins with another creature that's adapted to Hoth's frigid environment: the carnivorous wampa. When Han Solo finds Luke, it's after the young Jedi and his tauntaun have been attacked by a wampa. While Luke survives, his tauntaun sadly doesn't, and Han Solo uses the animal to keep them both warm until he is able to construct a shelter for them.

This Tauntaun Cowl is a cosy and much better smelling way to keep warm during winter storms. The cowl is worked in two layers—a base of worsted weight yarn, followed by a fuzzier yarn layer for added warmth. To create the ideal texture, you will use three sizes of crochet hooks throughout the project. The small and medium hooks are used for the first layer: the smallest for the foundation ribbing and the medium-sized hook for the main body of the cowl. Finally, the largest hook creates the fuzzy outer layer, allowing for a soft, thick, and warm finish that captures the coziness of a tauntaun's fur.

> "THERE ISN'T ENOUGH LIFE ON THIS ICE CUBE TO FILL A SPACE CRUISER. SENSORS ARE PLACED. I'M GOING BACK."
>
> —Han Solo, *The Empire Strikes Back*

SIZES
Adult Small (Adult Large)

FINISHED MEASUREMENTS
Height: 18 in. / 46 cm (both sizes)
Circumference: 23 (28) in. / 58.5 (71) cm
Sample shown in Adult Small.

YARN
Worsted weight (medium #4) shown in Lion Brand Yarn *Heartland* (100% Acrylic, 251 yd. / 230 m per 5 oz. / 142 g ball)
Colour A: #136-152AG White Sands, 2 (2) balls / 330 (395) yd. / 302 (361) m
Super Bulky weight (super bulky #6) shown in Lion Brand Yarn *Go for Faux* (100% Polyester, 60 yd. / 65 m per 3½ oz. / 100 g ball)
Colour B: #322-204BH Chinchilla, 1 (2) ball(s) / 51 (63) yd. / 47 (58) m

HOOKS
US H-8 / 5.00 mm crochet hook
US J-10 / 6.00 mm crochet hook (main hook), or *size needed to obtain gauge*
US M-13 / 9.00 mm crochet hook

NOTIONS
Tapestry needle
Locking stitch markers

GAUGE
With US J-10 / 6.00 mm crochet hook and A, 14 sts and 9 rnds = 4 in. / 10 cm in pattern, unblocked
Make sure to check your gauge.

SPECIAL STITCHES

- **Surface Slip Stitch:** Worked in the chain spaces created in the Main Body of the cowl. Holding working yarn inside the cowl, insert hook into first ch sp, yarn over and pull up a loop, insert hook into next ch sp, *yarn over and pull up a loop, draw yarn through loop on hook to complete the sl st. Insert hook into next chain space and repeat from *.

- **TIP:** Keep these stitches very loose, or you risk tightening the cowl so much it will no longer fit over your head. If you've never used this technique before, a few practice rows will be beneficial to help you get the correct tension.

INSPIRED CLOTHING

PATTERN NOTES

- Ribbing is worked first, back and forth in rows.
- Main Body is worked in continuous rounds, without joining.
- In Main Body, the RS is always facing you.
- Adjust the height of the cowl by working fewer or more rounds in Main Body section in multiples of two rnds. Such adjustments will affect the required yardage for both yarns.
- Fur is applied using Surface Slip Stitches.

RIBBING

With **A** and US H-8 / 5.00 mm crochet hook.

Row 1: Ch 8 and, working in back bumps, sl st in second ch from hook and in each ch across, turn – 7 sts.

Row 2: Ch 1, sl st-blo in each st across, turn.

Rows 3–118 (142): Repeat Row 2.

Sew short ends together to form a ring. Do not fasten off.

MAIN BODY

With US J-10 / 6.00 mm crochet hook.

Begin working in Ribbing row ends.

Rnd 1 (working in the spaces between the ribs): Ch 1, *hdc in next 2 spaces, ch 1, rep from * around, do not join – 60 (72) hdc and 30 (36) ch sps.

Rnd 2: *Hdc next 2 sts, ch 1, skip ch sp, rep from * around – 60 (72) hdc and 30 (36) ch sps.

Rnds 3–33: Rep Rnd 2.

Rnd 34: Sc in each hdc and ch sp around, join with a sl st in first sc – 90 (108) sts.

Fasten off.

APPLY THE FUR

With **B** and US M-13 / 9.00 mm hook.

Locate the ch sp directly below the seam on the Ribbing, insert hook into this ch sp and pull up a loop. Work loosely in Surface Slip Stitch, placing last Surface Slip Stitch in same ch sp you started in, then continue to work in Surface Slip Stitch 2 rnds below.

Continue as established, working in Surface Slip Stitch every other rnd, to the bottom of the Cowl.

One round of unworked ch sps remains at the bottom of the Cowl.

After last round, fasten off and weave in ends.

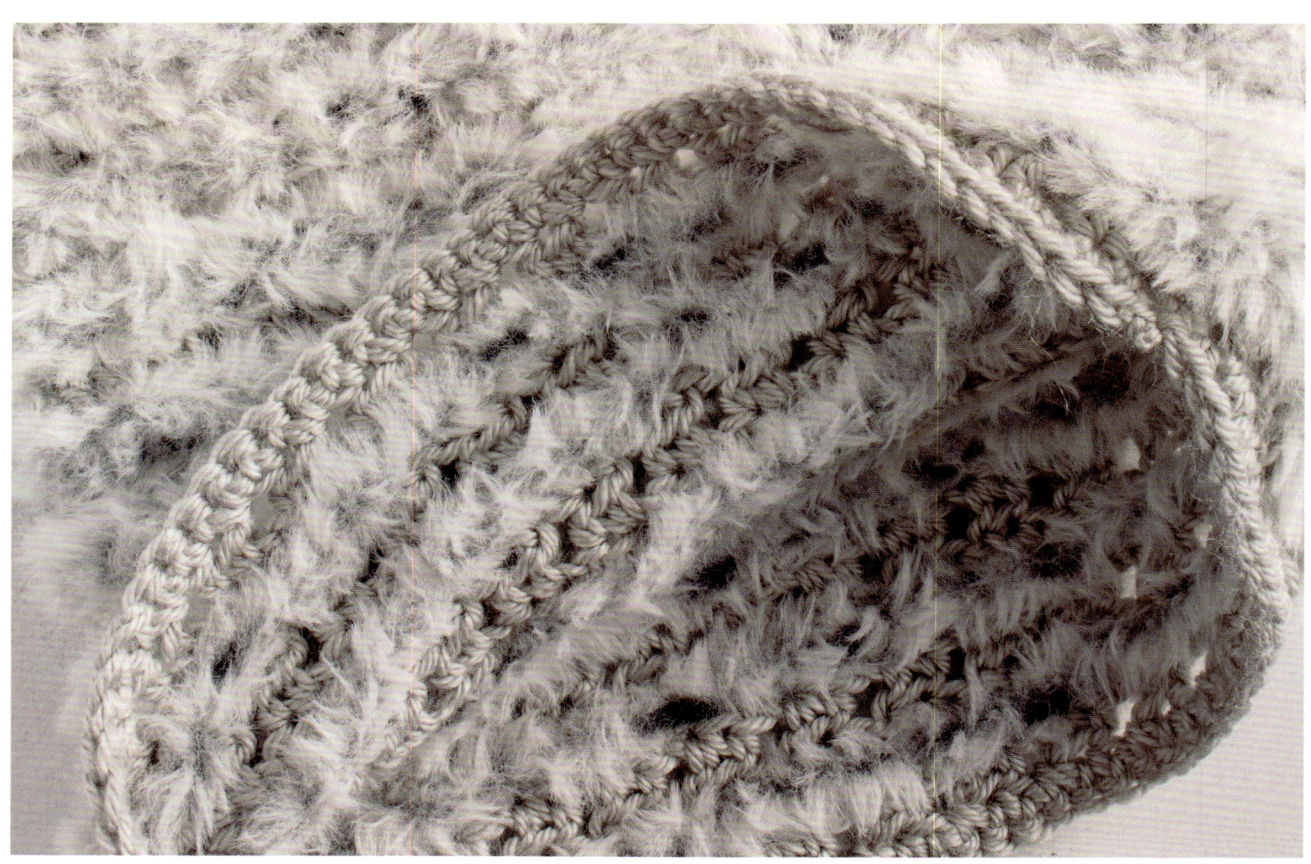

EWOK TOQUE

Designed by Leah Parker

SKILL LEVEL: ✎

Ewoks create their homes high up in the trees on the Forest Moon of Endor. Short, furry creatures, they are as resourceful as it comes—using traps to catch their food and wooden spears as weapons. They quickly adapt to new technology and new visitors, even befriending the Rebel Alliance's strike team, led by General Han Solo. Through their bravery and clever tactics, the Ewoks play a crucial role in helping the rebel crew secure a victory at the Battle of Endor.

Capture a bit of that Ewok ingenuity and create a sweet gift for the little ones in your life with this adorable, fluffy toque . . . or turn your whole community into an Ewok-inspired tribe by following the adjustable size instructions for this pattern. Just remember to work on the cap and ears separately, then join them together at the end. To give this toque that signature Ewok look, faux-fur yarn and a larger crochet hook are used.

> "I'M AFRAID OUR FURRY COMPANION HAS GONE AND DONE SOMETHING RATHER RASH."
>
> —C-3PO, *Return of the Jedi*

SIZES
Baby (Toddler, Child, Adult)

FINISHED MEASUREMENTS
Height: 6 (6.5, 7, 7.5) in. / 15 (16.5, 17.5, 19) cm, excluding faux fur trim.
Circumference: 16 (17.5, 19.3, 21) in. / 40.6 (44.5, 49, 53.5) cm
Sample is shown in size Toddler.

YARN
Super Bulky weight (super bulky #6) shown in Lion Brand Yarn *Wool Ease Thick and Quick* (80% Acrylic, 20% Wool, 106 yd. / 97 m per 6 oz. / 170 g ball)
Colour A: #640-135 Spice, 1 ball
Jumbo weight (jumbo #7) shown in Lion Brand Yarn *Go for Faux Thick and Quick* (100% Polyester, 24 yd. / 22 m per 4.2 oz. / 120 g ball)
Colour B: #323-209AT Chow Chow, 1 ball

HOOKS
US K-10½ / 6.5 mm crochet hook, or *size needed to obtain gauge*
US L-11 / 8.00 mm

NOTIONS
Locking stitch markers
Tapestry needle

GAUGE
With K-10½ / 6.5 mm crochet hook and **A**, 9 sts and 8 rows = 4 in. / 10 cm in hdc
Make sure to check your gauge.

SPECIAL STITCHES
- **Hdc2tog (half double crochet two together):** Yarn over, insert hook into next stitch and pull up a loop, yarn over, insert hook into next stitch and pull up a loop, yarn over and draw yarn through 5 loops on hook.

PATTERN NOTES
- Toque is crocheted from the bottom up, and shaped as you go. The fur detail along the bottom is worked after the main body of the toque is completed. The ears are worked separately and sewn on after.

INSPIRED CLOTHING

TOQUE

With K-10½ / 6.5 mm crochet hook and **A**, ch 36 (40, 44, 48).

Being careful not to twist, join with sl st in first ch.

Rnd 1: Ch 1, hdc in each st around, join with sl st in first st – 36 (40, 44, 48) sts.

Rnds 2–3: Rep Rnd 1.

Rnd 4: Ch 1, *hdc2tog, hdc in next 4 (6, 9, 10) sts, rep from * around, join with sl st in first st – 30 (35, 40, 44) sts.

Rnd 5: Ch 1, hdc in each st around, join with sl st in first st.

Rnd 6: Ch 1, *hdc2tog, hdc in next 3 (5, 8, 9) sts, rep from * around, join with sl st in first st – 24 (30, 36, 40) sts.

Rnd 7: Ch 1, hdc in each st around, join with sl st in first st.

Rnd 8: Ch 1, *hdc2tog, hdc in next 2 (4, 7, 8) sts, rep from * around, join with sl st in first st – 18 (25, 32, 36) sts.

Rnd 9: Ch 1, hdc in each st around, join with sl st in first st.

SIZE BABY ONLY

Rnd 10: Ch 1, hdc2tog around, join with sl st in first st – 9 sts.

Fasten off, leaving a long tail.

SIZE TODDLER ONLY

Rnd 10: Ch 1, *hdc2tog, hdc in next 3 sts, rep from * around, join with sl st in first st – 20 sts.

Rnd 11: Ch 1, *hdc2tog, hdc in next 2 sts, rep from * around, join with sl st in first st – 15 sts.

Rnd 12: Ch 1, hdc2tog around, until 1 st remains, hdc in next, join with sl st in first st – 8 hdc.

Fasten off, leaving a long tail.

SIZES CHILD (ADULT)

Rnd 10: Ch 1, *hdc2tog, hdc in next 6 (7) sts, rep from * around, join with sl st in first st – 28 (32) sts.

Rnd 11: Ch 1, *hdc2tog, hdc in next 5 (6) sts, rep from * around, join with sl st in first st – 24 (28) sts.

Rnd 12: Ch 1, *hdc2tog, hdc in next 4 (5) sts, rep from * around, join with sl st in first st – 20 (24) sts.

Rnd 13: Ch 1, *hdc2tog, hdc in next 3 (4) sts, rep from * around, join with sl st in first st – 16 (20) sts.

SIZE CHILD ONLY

Rnd 14: Ch 1, hdc2tog around, join with sl st in first st – 8 sts.

Fasten off, leaving a long tail.

SIZE ADULT ONLY

Rnd 14: Ch 1, *hdc2tog, hdc in next 3 sts, rep from * around, join with sl st in first st – 16 sts.

Rnd 15: Ch 1, hdc2tog around, join with sl st in first st – 8 sts.

Fasten off, leaving a long tail.

FAUX FUR TRIM (ALL SIZES)

With US L-11 / 8.00 mm crochet hook and **B**, join yarn at bottom of Toque.

Rnd 1: Ch 1, hdc in each st around, join with sl st in first st – 36 (40, 44, 48) sts.

Fasten off and weave in ends.

EARS (MAKE 2)

With US L-11 / 8.00 mm crochet hook and **B**.

Row 1: Ch 3 (do not count as a st), 5 hdc in first ch – 5 sts.

Row 2: Ch 1, turn, *2 hdc in next st, hdc in next, rep from * once, 2 hdc in last – 8 sts.

Fasten off, leaving a long tail for sewing.

FINISHING

Weave long tail through remaining sts at the top of the Toque and pull tight to close the hole.

Pin Ears on Toque, approximately 6 in. / 15 cm apart. Sew in place.

Weave in ends.

HANDMAIDEN-INSPIRED JUMPER

Designed by Leah Parker

SKILL LEVEL: ///

The Naboo Royal Handmaidens are a group of young women chosen as aides to Queen Amidala. They take up a range of roles in their service, acting as wardrobe attendants, bodyguards, political aides, decoys, and companions. Their day-to-day outfits are typically chosen to complement the queen's, and often incorporate hoods that hide their faces. While handmaidens traditionally serve royal leaders, those loyal to Amidala remain at her side when she becomes senator to Naboo. One brave handmaiden, Cordé, acts as a decoy for Amidala and loses her own life when an assassination attempt is made to prevent the senator from voting against the Galactic Republic's Military Creation Act.

This jumper is inspired by the vibrant robes worn by the Naboo Royal Handmaidens in *The Phantom Menace*. A beautiful gradient of yellows, reds, and oranges blends together with a striking simplicity that's not to be underestimated. If this is your first time crocheting a jumper, don't let the prospect overwhelm you. The basic stitch pattern is easy to work through while the range of colours will give the finished project the appearance of a much more complicated piece.

> "YOUR HONOUR, I AM QUEEN AMIDALA. THIS IS MY DECOY, MY PROTECTION . . . MY LOYAL BODYGUARD."
>
> — Padmé Amidala, *The Phantom Menace*

SIZES
XS (S, M, L, XL, 2X, 3X, 4X, 5X)
Instructions are written for the smallest size, with larger sizes given in parentheses; when only one number or set of instructions is given, it applies to all sizes.

FINISHED MEASUREMENTS
Chest circumference: 33.5 (37, 40.5, 45, 48, 52.5, 58, 61, 65.5) in. / 85 (94, 103, 114.5, 122, 133.5, 147.5, 155, 166.5) cm
Sleeve Length: 12 (12, 12, 14, 14, 14, 16, 16, 16) in. / 30.5 (30.5, 30.5, 35.5, 35.5, 35.5, 40.5, 40.5, 40.5) cm
Armhole Depth: 9 (9, 10, 10, 11, 11, 12, 12, 13) in. / 23 (23, 25.5, 25.5, 28, 28, 30.5, 30.5, 33) cm
Sample is shown in size XL.

YARN
DK weight (light #3) shown in Ancient Arts Yarns *Nettle Soft DK* (68% Superwash Merino, 32% Nettle, 263 yd. / 240 m per 3.5 oz. / 100 g skein)
Colour A: Cranberry 1 (1, 2, 2, 2, 2, 2, 2, 2) skeins
Colour B: Nectarine 1 (2, 2, 2, 2, 2, 2, 3, 3) skeins
Colour C: Gold Mine 2 (2, 2, 2, 3, 3, 3, 3, 4) skeins
Colour D: Golden Retriever 1 (1, 2, 2, 2, 2, 2, 2, 3) skeins

HOOKS
US G / 4.25 mm crochet hook
US 7 / 4.50 mm crochet hook, or *size needed to obtain gauge*

NOTIONS
Tapestry needle
9 locking stitch markers

GAUGE
With US 7 / 4.50 mm crochet hook, 14 sts and 14 rnds = 4 in. / 10 cm in hdc.
Make sure to check your gauge.

SPECIAL ABBREVIATIONS
- **Hdc2tog (half double crochet two together):** Yarn over, insert hook into next stitch and pull up a loop, yarn over, insert hook into next stitch and pull up a loop, yarn over and draw yarn through 5 loops on hook.

INSPIRED CLOTHING

PATTERN NOTES

- The jumper is worked top down in the round with a circular yoke and gradual increases. It is then separated for the body and the sleeves.
- Each sleeve is worked top down individually.
- Change colour by making the last "yarn over, pull through" of the stitch with the new colour.
- To lengthen or shorten the body, crochet more or fewer rounds using the colour of your choice. This will change the amount of yarn required.
- To lengthen or shorten the sleeves, crochet more or fewer rounds within the sections noted in the pattern. This will change the amount of yarn required.
- The jumper is designed to be worn with approximately 4 in. / 10 cm of positive ease.

NECK BAND

With US G / 4.25 mm crochet hook and **A**, ch 9.

Row 1: Sc in second ch from hook and in each ch across – 8 sc.

Row 2: Turn, ch 1, sc-blo in each st across.

Rows 3–72 (80, 88, 88, 88, 96, 96, 104, 104): Rep Row 2.

Join first and last rows with sl sts to form a ring.

Do not fasten off.

YOKE

With US 7 / 4.50 mm crochet hook.

Rnd 1: Ch 1, hdc in each row end of Neck Band, sl st in first st to join – 72 (80, 88, 88, 88, 96, 96, 104, 104) hdc.

Rnd 2: *Hdc in next 9 (10, 11, 11, 11, 12, 12, 13, 13) sts, pm, rep from * around, sl st in first st to join.

Rnd 3: *Hdc in each st around to marker, 2 hdc in marked st, pm, rep from * around, sl st in first st to join – 80 (88, 96, 96, 96, 104, 104, 112, 112) hdc.

Rnds 4–18 (19, 20, 23, 26, 28, 32, 33, 35): Rep Rnd 3 – 200 (216, 232, 256, 280, 304, 336, 352, 368) hdc.

Rnd 19 (20, 21, 24, 27, 29, 33, 34, 36): With **B**, ch 1, hdc in each st around, evenly spacing 2 (2, 2, 2, 0, 4, 4, 6, 6) increases, sl st in first st to join – 202 (218, 234, 258, 280, 308, 340, 358, 374) hdc.

Rnds 20–32 (21–32, 22–36, 25–36, 28–40, 30–40, 34–42, 35–42, 37–46): Ch 1, hdc in each st around, sl st in first st to join.

SEPARATE BODY AND SLEEVES

Next rnd: Skip 42 (44, 46, 50, 56, 62, 68, 72, 72) sts, hdc in next 54 (62, 68, 74, 78, 84, 94, 100, 108) for the back, skip 42 (44, 46, 50, 56, 62, 68, 72, 72) sts, hdc in next 64 (68, 74, 84, 90, 100, 110, 114, 122) for the front – 118 (130, 142, 158, 168, 184, 204, 214, 230) sts.

Stitches that are skipped in this rnd are left aside for the Sleeves.

BODY

Rnd 1: With **B**, ch 1, hdc in each st around, sl st in first st to join – 118 (130, 142, 158, 168, 184, 204, 214, 230) hdc.

Rnds 2–5: Rep Rnd 1.

Rnds 6–30: With **C**, rep Rnd 1.

Rnds 31–42: With **D**, rep Rnd 1.

Add or subtract rows in this section for a longer or shorter Body.

Fasten off.

BODY RIBBING

With US G / 4.25 mm crochet hook and **D**, ch 9.

Row 1: Sc in second ch from hook and in each ch across – 8 sc.

Row 2: Turn, ch 1, sc-blo in each st across.

Rows 3–118 (130, 142, 158, 168, 184, 204, 214, 230): Rep Row 2.

Join first and last rows with sl sts to form a ring.

Do not fasten off.

Rnd 1: Ch 1, sc in each row end of Ribbing, sl st to join – 118 (130, 142, 158, 168, 184, 204, 214, 230) hdc.

Fasten off. Sew Ribbing onto bottom of the Body using whip stitch.

SLEEVES

SIZES XS-L

With US 7 / 4.50 mm crochet hook, join **B** to bottom of arm opening.

Rnd 1: Ch 1, hdc in each st around arm opening, sl st in first st to join – 42 (44, 46, 50) hdc.

Rnds 2–4: Ch 1, hdc in each st around, sl st in first st to join.

Rnd 5: Ch 1, hdc2tog in first 2 sts, hdc in each st around until 2 sts remain, hdc2tog in last 2 sts, sl st in first st to join – 40 (42, 44, 48) hdc.

Rnds 6–21 (25, 29, 29): With **C**, rep Rnds 2–5 – 32 (32, 32, 36) hdc remain.

Rnds 22–33 (26–33, 30–33, 30–33): Ch 1, hdc in each st around, sl st in first st to join.

Rnds 34–42 (42, 42, 49): With **D**, ch 1, hdc in each st around, sl st in first st to join. Add or subtract rows in this section for a longer or shorter Sleeve.

Fasten off. Repeat for second Sleeve.

SIZE XL

With US 7 / 4.50 mm crochet hook, join **B** to bottom of arm opening.

Rnd 1: Ch 1, hdc in each st around arm opening, sl st in first st to join – 56 hdc.

Rnds 2–4: Ch 1, hdc in each st around, sl st in first st to join.

Rnd 5: Ch 1, hdc2tog in first 2 sts, hdc in each st around until 2 sts remain, hdc2tog in last 2 sts, sl st in first st to join – 54 hdc.

Rnds 6–33: With **C**, rep Rnds 2–5 – 40 hdc remain.

Rnds 34–41: With **D**, rep Rnds 2–5 –

36 hdc remain.

Rnds 42–49: Ch 1, hdc in each st around, sl st in first st to join.

Add or subtract rows in this section for a longer or shorter Sleeve.

Fasten off. Repeat for second Sleeve.

SIZE 2X

With US 7 / 4.50 mm crochet hook, join **B** to bottom of arm opening.

Rnd 1: Ch 1, hdc in each st around arm opening, sl st in first st to join – 62 hdc.

Rnds 2–3: Ch 1, hdc in each st around, sl st in first st to join.

Rnd 4: Ch 1, hdc2tog in first 2 sts, hdc in each st around until 2 sts remain, hdc2tog in last 2 sts, sl st in first st to join – 60 hdc.

Rnds 5–6: Rep Rnds 2–3.

Rnd 7: With **C**, rep Rnd 4 – 58 hdc remain.

Rnds 8–33: Rep Rnds 2–4, ending on a rep of Rnd 3 – 42 hdc remain.

Rnd 34: With **D**, rep Rnd 4 – 40 hdc remain.

Rnds 35–40: With **D**, rep Rnds 2–4 – 36 hdc.

Rnds 41–49: Ch 1, hdc in each st around, sl st in first st to join.

Add or subtract rows in this section for a longer or shorter Sleeve.

Fasten off. Repeat for second Sleeve.

SIZES 3X–5X

With US 7 / 4.50 mm crochet hook, join **B** to bottom of arm opening.

Rnd 1: Ch 1, hdc in each st around arm opening, sl st in first st to join – 68 (72, 72) hdc.

Rnd 2: Ch 1, hdc in each st around, sl st in first st to join.

Rnd 3: Ch 1, hdc2tog in first 2 sts, hdc in each st around until 2 sts remain, hdc2tog in last 2 sts, sl st in first st to join – 66 (70, 70) hdc.

Rnds 4–5: Rep Rnds 2–3 – 64 (68, 68) hdc.

Rnd 6: Rep Rnd 2.

Rnd 7: With **C**, rep Rnd 3 – 62 (66, 66) hdc.

Rnds 8–31 (35, 35): Rep Rnds 2–3 – 38 (38, 38) hdc remain.

Size 3X Only **Rnds 32–33:** Ch 1, hdc in each st around, sl st in first st to join.

Rnds 34–56 (36–56, 36–56): With **D**, ch 1, hdc in each st around, sl st in first st to join.

Add or subtract rows in this section for a longer or shorter Sleeve.

Fasten off. Repeat for second Sleeve.

CUFF (MAKE 2)

With US G / 4.25 mm crochet hook and **D**, ch 9.

Row 1: Sc in second ch from hook and in each ch across – 8 sc.

Row 2: Turn, ch 1, sc-blo in each st across.

Rows 3–32 (32, 32, 36, 36, 36, 38, 38, 38): Rep Row 2.

Join first and last rows with sl sts to form a ring.

Do not fasten off.

Rnd 1: Ch 1, sc in each row end of Cuff, sl st to join – 32 (32, 32, 36, 36, 36, 38, 38, 38) hdc.

Fasten off. Sew Cuff onto bottom of the Sleeve using whip stitch.

Weave in ends.

LONG HOODED SCARF

Designed by Kate Hammitt

SKILL LEVEL: ✎

The character Rey, typically referred to by first name alone, is introduced in *Star Wars: Episode VII—The Force Awakens* as a former scavenger turned pilot and mechanic living on the planet Jakku. At a young age, she learned how to survive on her own and adapt quickly to new surroundings, instincts that serve her well when a chance encounter with the droid BB-8 sends her life in a new direction. Teaming up with the First Order stormtrooper Finn, Rey helps bring BB-8's star chart to the Resistance, and with it, a clue to the whereabouts of Jedi Master Luke Skywalker. Originally hesitant about the pull she feels from the Force, Rey begins to embrace her rapidly growing powers, eventually taking up Luke Skywalker's lightsaber, as well as the quest to find him.

This scarf is inspired by the shape of the hooded wrap that Rey wears to protect herself from extreme weather, ranging from sandstorms to the beating sun. She appears in many different colours throughout the sequel trilogy, from tan on the desert planet of Jakku to white among the Death Star wreckage on the ocean moon Kef Bir. However, the colour photographed for this project is inspired by *Star Wars: Episode VIII—The Last Jedi*. When Rey and Kylo Ren face the Supreme Leader Snoke, Rey's outfit is a dark grey, almost black. This pattern includes alternate yarn colour suggestions, so you can choose which of Rey's looks you'd like to draw on—perfect for when you want to embrace your own connection to the Force, whether light or dark . . .

SIZE
One size

FINISHED MEASUREMENTS
SCARF:
Length: 168 in. / 427 cm
Width: 10 in. / 25.5 cm
HOOD:
Length: 10 in. / 25.5 cm
Width: 12 in. / 30.5 cm

YARN
Worsted weight (medium #4) shown in Lion Brand Yarn *Heartland* (100% Acrylic, 251 yd. / 230 m per 5 oz. / 142 g ball): 5 balls in #136-153Q Black Canyon.
Alternate colour suggestions: Lion Brand Yarn *Heartland* Acadia #136-098U or Grand Canyon #136-122G

HOOK
US J-10 / 6.00 mm crochet hook, or *size needed to obtain gauge*

NOTIONS
Tapestry needle
Locking stitch markers

GAUGE
16 sts and 15 rows = 4 in. / 10 cm in pattern, blocked.
Make sure to check your gauge.

PATTERN NOTES
- Crocheted in single crochet mesh stitch, this is a beginner-friendly pattern featuring a reversible fabric.
- Scarf is worked back and forth in rows.
- Hood is crocheted onto the centre of the Scarf, also in rows. No seaming is required.
- To customize the length or width of the Scarf, add or subtract 4 stitches or rows for every 1 in. / 2.5 cm desired.

"THE DARK SIDE IS IN OUR NATURE."

—Kylo Ren to Rey, *The Rise of Skywalker*

INSPIRED CLOTHING

SCARF

Row 1: Ch 40, sc in second ch from hook, *ch 1, sk 1, sc in next ch, rep from * to end – 39 sts.

Row 2: Ch 1, turn, sc in first st, *ch 1, sk 1, sc in next st, rep from * to end.

Rows 3–630: Rep Row 2 until Scarf measures 168 in. / 427 cm, or desired length.

Fasten off.

Tip: Place a stitch marker at the edge of Row 315 to mark row end where Hood begins.

HOOD

Join yarn in marked row end. Alternatively, fold Scarf in half to find the centre.

Row 1: Ch 40, sc in second ch from hook, *ch 1, sk 1, sc in next st, rep from * across – 39 sts.

Row 2: Sl st in next 2 row ends of Scarf, turn, sk both sl sts, sc in next st, *ch 1, sk 1, sc in next, rep from * across. Ch 1, now working on the opposite side of the starting chain, sc in next st, *ch 1, sk 1, sc in next, rep from * across – 78 sts (excluding sl sts).

Row 3: Sl st in next two row ends of Scarf, turn, sk both sl sts, sc in next st, *ch 1, sk 1, sc in next st, rep from * across – 78 sts.

Repeat Row 3 until Hood measures 12 in. / 30.5 cm or desired depth.

Fasten off.

FINISHING

Weave in ends. Block to finished measurements.

"I AM ALL THE JEDI."

—Rey, *The Rise of Skywalker*

GROGU BONNET

Designed by Romina Barlaro

SKILL LEVEL: ✦✦

Grogu is a youngling at the Jedi Temple on Coruscant, until Order 66 forces him into hiding. That's when he crosses paths with bounty hunter Din Djarin, who has been hired to retrieve the child by a mysterious Imperial known as "the Client." When Din, often referred to as Mando, learns what the Imperials have planned for Grogu, he decides to protect the child instead of turning him over. On the run from other bounty hunters, the pair travel the galaxy together looking for Jedi who can help train Grogu. Along the way, the pair form a deep bond, with Din taking on a father-figure role for Grogu.

In the spirit of this duo's sweet connection, this bonnet is a cosy covering for any child in your life. The pattern includes directions for baby-, toddler-, or child-sized bonnets. Whatever age the wearer of this Grogu-inspired bonnet, they'll no doubt be the cutest creature in the galaxy. And the soft, breathable yarn, meant to balance everyday comfort in warmer months with protection against chillier days in cooler ones, makes this adorable cap the cherry on top of any outfit. The bonnet is worked starting with a flat flap for the back of the head, around which the rest of the hat is then crocheted. The ears are crocheted separately and sewn onto the sides. The design captures Grogu's charm and offers a cosy, comfortable fit for any little one's adventures.

"THIS IS THE WAY."

—Din Djarin, *The Mandalorian*

SIZES
Baby (Toddler, Child)

To fit head circumference: 14–16 (16–17, 18–19) in. / 36–40.5 (40.5–43, 46–48) cm

For accurate sizing, measure the recipient's head circumference.

FINISHED MEASUREMENTS
Height: 7 (8, 9) in. / 18 (20, 23) cm, laid flat

Depth: 6 (7, 8) in. / 15 (18, 20) cm, laid flat

YARN
Jumbo weight (jumbo #7) shown in Bernat *Blanket Yarn* (100% Polyester, 97 yd. / 87 m per 10½ oz. / 300 g ball): 1 (2, 2) balls / 82 (98, 109) yd. / 75 (90, 100) m in Smoky Green.

HOOK
US K-10½ / 6.5 mm crochet hook, or *size needed to obtain gauge*

NOTIONS
Tapestry needle
Locking stitch markers

GAUGE
8 sts and 9 rows = 4 in. / 10 cm in sc
Make sure to check your gauge.

PATTERN NOTES
- Back of Bonnet is crocheted first. Stitches are then picked up around the Flap to crochet the Bonnet in single crochet rows.
- Ties and Ears are crocheted separately and attached to the Bonnet.

BACK OF BONNET

Row 1: Ch 6 (8, 10), sc in second ch from hook and in each ch across, turn – 5 (7, 9) sts.

Row 2: Ch 1, sc in each st across, turn.

Repeat Row 2 until Back of Bonnet measures 4 (5, 5.5) in. / 10 (13, 14) cm.

Do not fasten off.

BONNET

Stitches will now be picked up around Back of Bonnet.

Turn your work to crochet in row ends, then in the starting chain, and finally in opposite row ends.

Row 1: Ch 1, evenly sc 11 (12, 13) in row ends, sc in 6 (8, 10) starting chs, evenly sc 11 (12, 13) in row ends, turn – 28 (32, 36) sts.

Now working in rows across 3 sides.

Row 2: Ch 1, sc in each st across, turn – 28 (32, 36) sts.

Repeat Row 2 until Bonnet measures 6 (7, 8) in. / 15 (18, 20) cm from Row 1.

Fasten off and weave in ends.

TIES (MAKE 2)

Join yarn at bottom front corner of Bonnet.

Row 1: Ch 17, fasten off and weave in ends.

Repeat on second side.

EARS (MAKE 2)

Row 1: Ch 17, sc in second ch from hook and in each ch across, turn – 16 sts.

Rows 2–4: Ch 1, sc in each st across, turn.

Rows 5–6: Ch 1, sc2tog, sc in each st until 2 sts remain, sc2tog, turn – 12 sc.

Row 7: Ch 1, sc in each st across, turn.

Rows 8–9: Ch 1, sc2tog, sc in each st until 2 sts remain, sc2tog, turn – 8 sc.

Row 10: Ch 1, sc in each st across, turn.

Rows 11–12: Ch 1, sc2tog, sc in each st until 2 sts remain, sc2tog, turn – 4 sc.

Row 13: Ch 1, sc in each st across, turn.

Row 14: Ch 1, sc2tog twice – 2 sc.

Fasten off, leaving a long tail for sewing.

SHAPE THE EARS

Fold Ear in half lengthwise and sew through both thicknesses across long side.

Fold both bottom corners toward the centre and sew in place.

ASSEMBLY

Attach the Ears to the Bonnet approximately 2.5 in. / 6.5 cm from the bottom and 2.5 in. / 6.5 cm from the front of the Hat. To prevent the Ears from drooping, make a few stitches from the top of the Ears to the Bonnet to prop them up.

Weave in all ends and block lightly.

CHEWBACCA BANDOLIER SCARF

Designed by Leah Parker

SKILL LEVEL: ✎ ✎ ✎

Chewbacca, affectionately known as "Chewie" among his closest friends, is a Wookiee from the forested planet of Kashyyyk. He is the loyal co-pilot to Han Solo aboard the *Millennium Falcon*. A smuggler, a skilled mechanic, and a rebel, Chewie is known to be ready for a fight when it comes to friendship and honour. It's no wonder the character was inspired by director George Lucas's own loyal companion, an Alaskan malamute named Indiana. The giant, lovable dog made it a habit to sit in the passenger seat of Lucas's car, just like a trusted co-pilot.

This scarf is inspired by the bandolier of Chewie's iconic knapsack, which he is rarely seen without. It'll keep you just as prepared to face the cold as Chewie is to face an urgent repair on the *Millennium Falcon*. A great introduction to crochet colourwork, the bandolier pattern is formed using a combination of solid contrasting stitches. The scarf is crocheted back and forth in rows, and colour changes are worked seamlessly into the design. An easily transportable project, this is a fun one to try out if you find yourself in the co-pilot's seat on your next road trip!

"IT'S NOT WISE TO UPSET A WOOKIEE."

—Han Solo, *A New Hope*

SIZE
One size

FINISHED MEASUREMENTS
Length: 77 in. / 195 cm
Width: 8 in. / 20 cm

YARN
Worsted weight (medium #4) shown in Lion Brand Yarn *Heartland* (100% Acrylic, 251 yd. / 230 m per 5 oz. / 142 g ball)
Colour A: #136-126U Sequoia, 2 balls
Colour B: #136-099Q Dry Tortugas, 1 ball

HOOK
US J-10 / 6.00 mm crochet hook, or *size needed to obtain gauge*

NOTIONS
Tapestry needle
Locking stitch markers
Bobbins (optional)

GAUGE
12 sts by 10 rows = 4 in. / 10 cm in hdc
Make sure to check your gauge.

PATTERN NOTES
- Drop colour when not in use. The intarsia colourwork can be worked using bobbins, or carrying the yarn, or a combination of both.
- For rows between colourwork, you can carry **B** on the WS of the scarf or fasten off and join again when needed. If **B** is carried it will be visible on WS.

INSPIRED CLOTHING

PATTERN

To follow the graph:

With **A**, ch 26, then follow the graph from the bottom up.

Once you reach the top of the graph, repeat Rows 13–38, 5 times.

Repeat Rows 13–24 once.

Repeat Rows 2–12 once.

Row 1 (RS): With **A**, ch 26, hdc in third ch from hook and in each ch across – 24 sts.

Rows 2–12: Ch 1, turn, hdc in each st across.

Rows 13–24: Ch 1, turn, hdc in next 4 sts; with **B**, hdc in next 6; with **A**, hdc in next 4; with **B**, hdc in next 6; with **A**, hdc in next 4 – 24 sts.

Rows 25–28: Ch 1, turn, hdc in each st across.

Rows 29–34: Ch 1, turn, hdc in next 4 sts; with **B**, hdc in next 6; with **A**, hdc in next 4; with **B**, hdc in next 6; with **A**, hdc in next 4 – 24 sts.

Rows 35–38: Ch 1, turn, hdc in each st across.

Rows 39–168: Rep Rows 13–38.

Rows 169–180: Ch 1, turn, hdc in next 4 sts; with **B**, hdc in next 6; with **A**, hdc in next 4; with **B**, hdc in next 6; with **A**, hdc in next 4 – 24 sts.

Rows 181–192: Ch 1, turn, hdc in each st across.

Fasten off and weave in ends.

BEHIND THE SCENES

Chewbacca was originally played by Peter Mayhew, who was cast in the role due in part to his 7' 3" (221 cm) stature.

CHART

KEY A B

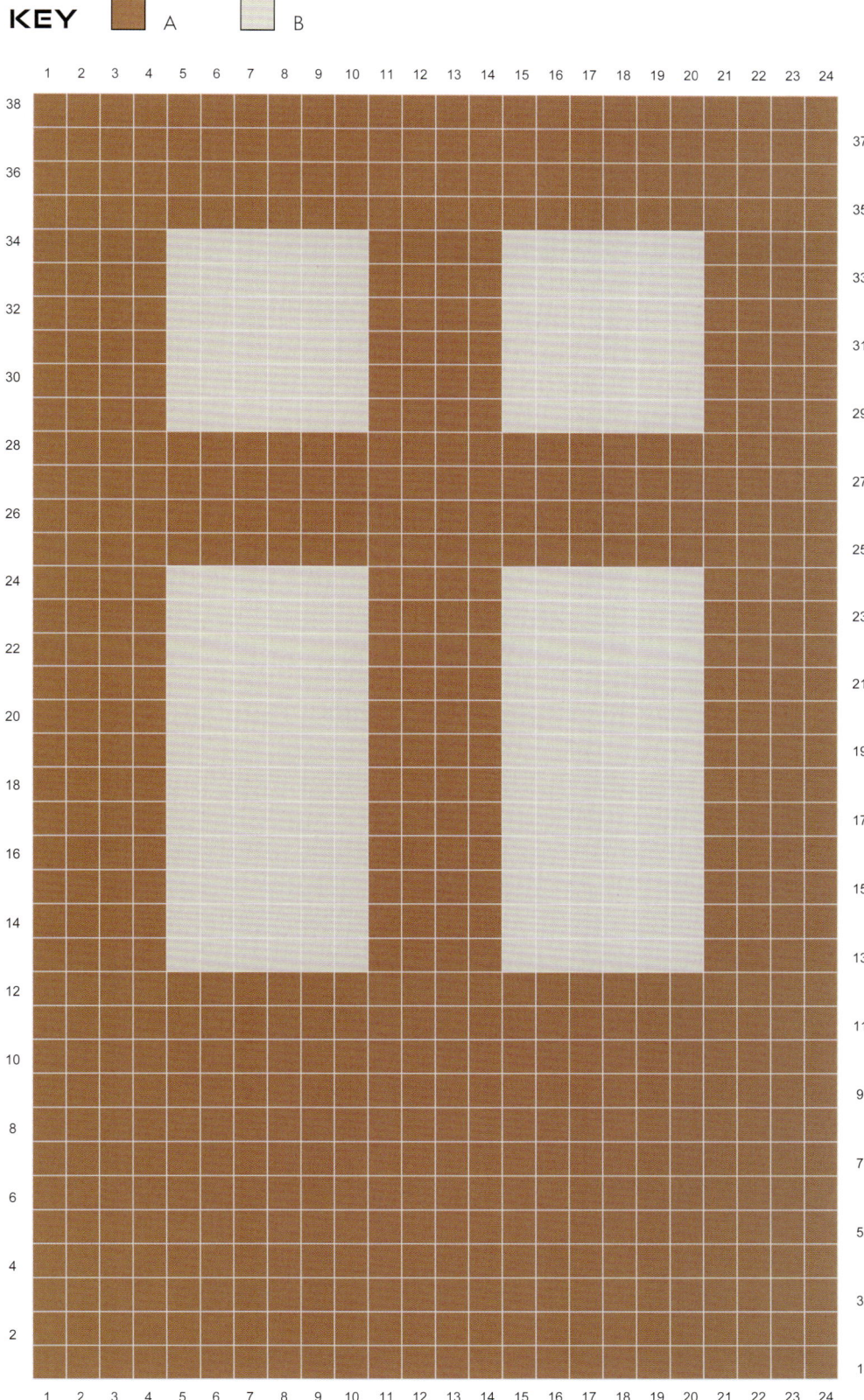

"LET THE WOOKIEE WIN."

—C-3PO, *A New Hope*

SECTION 4

HOME DÉCOR & GIFTS

"THE BELONGING YOU SEEK IS NOT
BEHIND YOU . . . IT IS AHEAD."

—Maz Kanata, *The Force Awakens*

From Luke Skywalker to Rey, generations of Jedi have sought to understand their place in the world, and their role within the balance of the Force. When it comes to the world of crochet, you have the power to shape your world, and your space, to suit *you*. Each project in this final section of the book is a way to bring *Star Wars* into your home. Step onto a mat that warns "It's a trap." Snuggle up with a Tatooine-inspired blanket that captures the warmth and beauty of the planet's twin suns. And keep your tea toasty with a BB-8 tea cosy. Just remember that when it comes to your place, the Force can be felt all around you, if you choose to embrace it.

"IT'S A TRAP" BATH MAT

Designed by Janine Mudge

SKILL LEVEL: ✦✦✦

Admiral Ackbar is a Rebel Alliance commander and leader of the fleet at the Battle of Endor. Considered a brilliant tactician, Ackbar is wary of the adage "fight fire with fire." Instead, he tries to make considered decisions while overseeing military manoeuvres from the bridge of his ship, *Home One*. It may come as little surprise, then, that the admiral is the first to declare "It's a trap!" when the rebels discover a fully operational Death Star waiting near Endor.

Whether you're the sort to dive in or tread carefully, this "It's a Trap" Bath Mat has you covered. The pattern requires just two colours and includes both a chart and written instructions, so you can easily follow along as you crochet this unforgettable message. It uses the tapestry crochet technique, which means you'll be crocheting over your unused colour. So, if things don't go to plan, well, at least you know what you're getting yourself into! Just like Ackbar's meticulously planned strategies, the invisible colour changes used will ensure that your project will have clean, sharp lines and an even texture, making it as well-crafted as his decisive battle tactics.

LANDO CALRISSIAN: "PULL UP! ALL CRAFT, PULL UP!"
ADMIRAL ACKBAR: "TAKE EVASIVE ACTION! GREEN GROUP, STICK CLOSE TO HOLDING SECTION MV-7!"
OFFICER: "ADMIRAL! WE HAVE ENEMY SHIPS IN SECTOR 47!"
ADMIRAL ACKBAR: "IT'S A TRAP!"

—*Return of the Jedi*

SIZE
One size

FINISHED MEASUREMENTS
Height: 20 in. / 51 cm
Width: 25.5 in. / 65 cm

YARN
Worsted weight (medium #4), shown in Lion Brand Yarn *24/7 Cotton* (100% Mercerized Cotton, 186 yd. / 170 m per 3.5 oz. / 100 g ball)
Main colour (MC): #761-153 Black, 3 balls
Contrast colour (CC): #761-133 Tangerine, 1 ball

HOOK
US G-6 / 4.00 mm crochet hook, or *size needed to obtain gauge*

NOTIONS
Tapestry needle
Locking stitch markers
Blocking mat and pins or combs

GAUGE
18 sts and 18 rows = 4 in. /10 cm in sc, unblocked
Make sure to check your gauge.

PATTERN NOTES
- This pattern uses the tapestry crochet technique of crocheting over the unused colour, carrying it through the pattern to be easily picked up. Change colours by pulling the new colour through at the last step of the final stitch of the previous colour.
- Keep a relatively loose tension on the carried yarn, so that it doesn't pucker the rows. Check your carried yarn tension regularly to ensure there are no loose ends sticking out between stitches.
- The graph shows 1 sc per square and is worked from the bottom up.
- Odd-number rows are on the RS, worked from right to left on the chart. Even-number rows are on the WS, worked from left to right on the chart. Left-handed crocheters work in reverse: RS from left to right and WS from right to left.
- When working a RS row, hold the carried yarn to the back as much as possible. When working a WS row, hold the carried yarn to the front as much as possible.

HOME DÉCOR & GIFTS

PATTERN

To follow the graph:

With **MC**, ch 111, then follow the graph from the bottom up.

Alternatively, follow the written instructions:

Row 1 (RS): With **MC**, ch 111, sc in second ch from hook and in each ch across, turn – 110 sts.

Rows 2–4: Ch 1, sc in each st across, turn.

Rows 5–6: With **CC**, ch 1, sc in each st across, turn.

Rows 7–8: With **MC**, ch 1, sc in each st across, turn.

Rows 9–10: With **CC**, ch 1, sc in each st across, turn.

Rows 11–12: With **MC**, ch 1, sc in each st across, turn.

Row 13: With **CC**, ch 1, sc in each st across, turn.

Rows 14–16: With **MC**, ch 1, sc in each st across, turn.

Row 17: With **MC**, ch 1, sc in next 10; with **CC**, sc in next 2; with **MC**, sc in next 17; with **CC**, sc in next 4; with **MC**, st in next 5; with **CC**, sc in next 3; with **MC**, sc in next 12; with **CC**, sc in next 4; with **MC**, sc in next 5; with **CC**, sc in next 4; with **MC**, sc in next 9; with **CC**, sc in next 4; with **MC**, sc in next 11; with **CC**, sc in next 3; with **MC**, sc in next 17, turn.

Row 18: Ch 1, sc in next 16; with **CC**, sc in next 4; with **MC**, sc in next 11; with **CC**, sc in next 4; with **MC**, sc in next 9; with **CC**, sc in next 4; with **MC**, sc in next 5; with **CC**, sc in next 4; with **MC**, sc in next 11; with **CC**, sc in next 4; with **MC**, sc in next 5; with **CC**, sc in next 4; with **MC**, sc in next 17; with **CC**, sc in next 3; with **MC**, sc in next 9, turn.

Row 19: Ch 1, sc in next 9; with **CC**, sc in next 3; with **MC**, sc in next 17; with **CC**, sc in next 4; with **MC**, sc in next 6; with **CC**, sc in next 3; with **MC**, sc in next 11; with **CC**, sc in next 3; with **MC**, sc in next 7; with **CC**, sc in next 4; with **MC**, sc in next 8; with **CC**, sc in next 4; with **MC**, sc in next 11; with **CC**, sc in next 4; with **MC**, sc in next 16, turn.

Row 20: Ch 1, sc in next 16; with **CC**, sc in next 4; with **MC**, sc in next 11; with **CC**, sc in next 4; with **MC**, sc in next 8; with **CC**, sc in next 4; with **MC**, sc in next 7; with **CC**, sc in next 4; with **MC**, sc in next 10; with **CC**, sc in next 3; with **MC**, sc in next 6; with **CC**, sc in next 4; with **MC**, sc in next 17; with **CC**, sc in next 3; with **MC**, sc in next 9, turn.

Row 21: Ch 1, sc in next 29; with **CC**, sc in next 4; with **MC**, sc in next 6; with **CC**, sc in next 4; with **MC**, sc in next 9; with **CC**, sc in next 4; with **MC**, sc in next 8; with **CC**, sc in next 4; with **MC**, sc in next 7; with **CC**, sc in next 4; with **MC**, sc in next 11; with **CC**, sc in next 4; with **MC**, sc in next 16, turn.

Row 22: Ch 1, sc in next 16; with **CC**, sc in next 4; with **MC**, sc in next 11; with **CC**, sc in next 4; with **MC**, sc in next 7; with **CC**, sc in next 4; with **MC**, sc in next 9; with **CC**, sc in next 9; with **MC**, sc in next 3; with **CC**, sc in next 3; with **MC**, sc in next 7; with **CC**, sc in next 4; with **MC**, sc in next 29, turn.

Row 23: Ch 1, sc in next 29; with **CC**, sc in next 4; with **MC**, sc in next 7; with **CC**, sc in next 4; with **MC**, sc in next 2; with **CC**, sc in next 9; with **MC**, sc in next 10; with **CC**, sc in next 4; with **MC**, sc in next 6; with **CC**, sc in next 4; with **MC**, sc in next 11; with **CC**, sc in next 4; with **MC**, sc in next 16, turn.

Row 24: Ch 1, sc in next 16; with **CC**, sc in next 4; with **MC**, sc in next 11; with **CC**, sc in next 4; with **MC**, sc in next 6; with **CC**, sc in next 4; with **MC**, sc in next 10; with **CC**, sc in next 9; with **MC**, sc in next 2; with **CC**, sc in next 4; with **MC**, sc in next 7; with **CC**, sc in next 4; with **MC**, sc in next 17; with **CC**, sc in next 2; with **MC**, sc in next 10, turn.

Row 25: Ch 1, sc in next 10; with **CC**, sc in next 2; with **MC**, sc in next 17; with **CC**, sc in next 4; with **MC**, sc in next 8; with **CC**, sc in next 3; with **MC**, sc in next 3; with **CC**, sc in next 7; with **MC**, sc in next 11; with **CC**, sc in next 4; with **MC**, sc in next 6; with **CC**, sc in next 4; with **MC**, sc in next 11; with **CC**, sc in next 4; with **MC**, sc in next 16, turn.

Row 26: Ch 1, sc in next 16; with **CC**, sc in next 4; with **MC**, sc in next 11; with **CC**, sc in next 4; with **MC**, sc in next 5; with **CC**, sc in next 4; with **MC**, sc in next 12; with **CC**, sc in next 4; with **MC**, sc in next 5; with **CC**, sc in next 4; with **MC**, sc in next 8; with **CC**, sc in next 4; with **MC**, sc in next 17; with **CC**, sc in next 3; with **MC**, sc in next 9, turn.

Row 27: Ch 1, sc in next 9; with **CC**, sc in next 3; with **MC**, sc in next 9; with **CC**, sc in next 12; with **MC**, sc in next 8; with **CC**, sc in next 4; with **MC**, sc in next 5; with **CC**, sc in next 4; with **MC**, sc in next 12; with **CC**, sc in next 13; with **MC**, sc in next 11; with **CC**, sc in next 4; with **MC**, sc in next 16, turn.

Row 28: Ch 1, sc in next 16; with **CC**, sc in next 4; with **MC**, sc in next 11; with **CC**, sc in next 15; with **MC**, sc in next 11; with **CC**, sc in next 4; with **MC**, sc in next 4; with **CC**, sc in next 4; with **MC**, sc in next 8; with **CC**, sc in next 14; with **MC**, sc in next 7; with **CC**, sc in next 3; with **MC**, sc in next 9, turn.

Row 29: Ch 1, sc in next 9; with **CC**, sc in next 3; with **MC**, sc in next 6; with **CC**, sc in next 15; with **MC**, sc in next 9; with **CC**, sc in next 4; with **MC**, sc in next 3; with **CC**, sc in next 4; with **MC**, sc in next 11; with **CC**, sc in next 15; with **MC**, sc in next 11; with **CC**, sc in next 4; with **MC**, sc in next 16, turn.

Row 30: Ch 1, sc in next 16 with **CC**, sc in next 4; with **MC**, sc in next 11; with **CC**, sc in next 16; with **MC**, sc in next 10; with **CC**, sc in next 4; with **MC**, sc in next 3; with **CC**, sc in next 4; with **MC**, sc in next 9; with **CC**, sc in next 15; with **MC**, sc in next 6; with **CC**, sc in next 3; with **MC**, sc in next 9, turn.

Row 31: Ch 1, sc in next 9; with **CC**, sc in next 3; with **MC**, sc in next 6; with **CC**, sc in next 14; with **MC**, sc in next 10; with **CC**, sc in next 4; with **MC**, sc in next 3; with **CC**, sc in next 3; with **MC**, sc in next 11; with **CC**, sc in next 15; with **MC**, sc in next 12; with **CC**, sc in next 4; with **MC**, sc in next 16, turn.

Row 32: Ch 1, sc in next 16; with **CC**, sc in next 4; with **MC**, sc in next 23; with **CC**, sc in next 4; with **MC**, sc in next 11; with **CC**, sc in next 4; with **MC**, sc in next 2; with **CC**, sc in next 3; with **MC**, sc in next 22; with **CC**, sc in next 4; with **MC**, sc in next 5; with **CC**, sc in next 3; with **MC**, sc in next 9, turn.

Row 33: Ch 1, sc in next 9; with **CC**, sc in next 3; with **MC**, sc in next 5; with **CC**, sc in next 4; with **MC**, sc in next 22; with **CC**, sc in next 4; with **MC**, sc in next; with **CC**, sc in next 4; with **MC**, sc in next 10; with **CC**, sc in next 4; with **MC**, sc in next 24; with **CC**, sc in next 4; with **MC**, sc in next 16, turn.

Row 34: Ch 1, sc in next 16; with **CC**, sc in next 4; with **MC**, sc in next 24; with **CC**, sc in next 4; with **MC**, sc in next 10; with **CC**, sc in next 4; with **MC**, sc in next; with **CC**, sc in next 4; with **MC**, sc in next 22; with **CC**, sc in next 4; with **MC**, sc in next 5; with **CC**, sc in next 3; with **MC**, sc in next 9, turn.

Row 35: Ch 1, sc in next 9; with **CC**, sc in next 3; with **MC**, sc in next 5; with **CC**, sc in next 4; with **MC**, sc in next 23; with **CC**, sc in next 3; with **MC**, sc in next; with **CC**, sc in next 3; with **MC**, sc in next 11; with **CC**, sc in next 4; with **MC**, sc in next 24; with **CC**, sc in next 4; with **MC**, sc in next 16, turn.

Row 36: Ch 1, sc in next 16; with **CC**, sc in next 4; with **MC**, sc in next 23; with **CC**, sc in next 5; with **MC**, sc in next 11; with **CC**, sc in next 7; with **MC**, sc in next 22; with **CC**, sc in next 5; with **MC**, sc in next 5; with **CC**, sc in next 3; with **MC**, sc in next 9, turn.

Row 37: Ch 1, sc in next 9; with **CC**, sc in next 4; with **MC**, sc in next 5; with **CC**, sc in next 15; with **MC**, sc in next 11; with **CC**, sc in next 7; with **MC**, sc in next 12; with **CC**, sc in next 16; with **MC**, sc in next 5; with **CC**, sc in next 15; with **MC**, sc in next 11, turn.

Row 38: Ch 1, sc in next 10; with **CC**, sc in next 17; with **MC**, sc in next 4; with **CC**, sc in next 16; with **MC**, sc in next 13; with **CC**, sc in next 5; with **MC**, sc in next 12; with **CC**, sc in next 15; with **MC**, sc in next 5; with **CC**, sc in next 4; with **MC**, sc in next 9, turn.

Row 39: Ch 1, sc in next 9; with **CC**, sc in next 4; with **MC**, sc in next 5; with **CC**, sc in next 15; with **MC**, sc in next 12; with **CC**, sc in next 5; with **MC**, sc in next 13; with **CC**, sc in next 16; with **MC**, sc in next 4; with **CC**, sc in next 17; with **MC**, sc in next 10, turn.

Row 40: Ch 1, sc in next 10; with **CC**, sc in next 17; with **MC**, sc in next 4; with **CC**, sc in next 15; with **MC**, sc in next 14; with **CC**, sc in next 5; with **MC**, sc in next 12; with **CC**, sc in next 14; with **MC**, sc in next 6; with **CC**, sc in next 4; with **MC**, sc in next 9, turn.

Row 41: Ch 1, sc in next 9; with **CC**, sc in next 4; with **MC**, sc in next 7; with **CC**, sc in next 13; with **MC**, sc in next 13; with **CC**, sc in next 3; with **MC**, sc in next 16; with **CC**, sc in next 14; with **MC**, sc in next 5; with **CC**, sc in next 16; with **MC**, sc in next 10, turn.

Row 42: Ch 1, sc in next 97; with **CC**, sc in next 4; with **MC**, sc in next 9, turn.

Rows 43–48: With **MC**, ch 1, sc in each st across, turn.

Row 49: Ch 1, sc in next 12; with **CC**, sc in next 3; with **MC**, sc in next 12; with **CC**, sc in next 4; with **MC**, sc in next 20; with **CC**, sc in next 12; with **MC**, sc in next 16; with **CC**, sc in next 3; with **MC**, sc in next 12; with **CC**, sc in next 4; with **MC**, sc in next 12, turn.

Row 50: Ch 1, sc in next 12; with **CC**, sc in next 4; with **MC**, sc in next 11; with **CC**, sc in next 4; with **MC**, sc in next 15; with **CC**, sc in next 14; with **MC**, sc in next 19; with **CC**, sc in next 4; with **MC**, sc in next 11; with **CC**, sc in next 4; with **MC**, sc in next 12, turn.

Row 51: Ch 1, sc in next 13; with **CC**, sc in next 3; with **MC**, sc in next 11; with **CC**, sc in next 3; with **MC**, sc in next 19; with **CC**, sc in next 15; with **MC**, sc in next 15; with **CC**, sc in next 4; with **MC**, sc in next 11; with **CC**, sc in next 4; with **MC**, sc in next 12, turn.

Row 52: Ch 1, sc in next 12; with **CC**, sc in next 4; with **MC**, sc in next 11; with **CC**, sc in next 4; with **MC**, sc in next 15; with **CC**, sc in next 15; with **MC**, sc in next 19; with **CC**, sc in next 4; with **MC**, sc in next 10; with **CC**, sc in next 3; with **MC**, sc in next 13, turn.

Row 53: Ch 1, sc in next 13; with **CC**, sc in next 4; with **MC**, sc in next 9; with **CC**, sc in next 4; with **MC**, sc in next 19; with **CC**, sc in next 15; with **MC**, sc in next 15; with **CC**, sc in next 4; with **MC**, sc in next 11; with **CC**, sc in next 4; with **MC**, sc in next 12, turn.

Row 54: Ch 1, sc in next 12; with **CC**, sc in next 4; with **MC**, sc in next 11; with **CC**, sc in next 4; with **MC**, sc in next 27; with **CC**, sc in next 3; with **MC**, sc in next 20; with **CC**, sc in next 9; with **MC**, sc in next 3; with **CC**, sc in next 3; with **MC**, sc in next 14, turn.

Row 55: Ch 1, sc in next 14; with **CC**, sc in next 4; with **MC**, sc in next 2; with **CC**, sc in next 9; with **MC**, sc in next 20; with **CC**, sc in next 3; with **MC**, sc in next 27; with **CC**, sc in next 4; with **MC**, sc in next 11; with **CC**, sc in next 4; with **MC**, sc in next 12, turn.

Row 56: Ch 1, sc in next 12; with **CC**, sc in next 4; with **MC**, sc in next 11; with **CC**, sc in next 4; with **MC**, sc in next 27; with **CC**, sc in next 3; with **MC**, sc in next 20; with **CC**, sc in next 9; with **MC**, sc in next 2; with **CC**, sc in next 4; with **MC**, sc in next 14, turn.

Row 57: Ch 1, sc in next 15; with **CC**, sc in next 3; with **MC**, sc in next 3; with **CC**, sc in next 7; with **MC**, sc in next 21; with **CC**, sc in next 3; with **MC**, sc in next 27; with **CC**, sc in next 4; with **MC**, sc in next 11; with **CC**, sc in next 4; with **MC**, sc in next 12, turn.

Row 58: Ch 1, sc in next 12; with **CC**, sc in next 4; with **MC**, sc in next 11; with **CC**, sc in next 4; with **MC**, sc in next 27; with **CC**, sc in next 3; with **MC**, sc in next 21; with **CC**, sc in next 4; with **MC**, sc in next 6; with **CC**, sc in next 3; with **MC**, sc in next 15, turn.

Row 59: Ch 1, sc in next 15; with **CC**, sc in next 4; with **MC**, sc in next 5; with **CC**, sc in next 4; with **MC**, sc in next 21; with **CC**, sc in next 13; with **MC**, sc in next 17; with **CC**, sc in next 4; with **MC**, sc in next 11; with **CC**, sc in next 4; with **MC**, sc in next 12, turn.

Row 60: Ch 1, sc in next 12; with **CC**, sc in next 4; with **MC**, sc in next 11; with **CC**, sc in next 4; with **MC**, sc in next 16; with **CC**, sc in next 14; with **MC**, sc in next 22; with **CC**, sc in next 4; with **MC**, sc in next 4; with **CC**, sc in next 4; with **MC**, sc in next 15, turn.

Row 61: Ch 1, sc in next 16; with **CC**, sc in next 3; with **MC**, sc in next 4; with **CC**, sc in next 4; with **MC**, sc in next 22; with **CC**, sc in next 14; with **MC**, sc in next 16; with **CC**, sc in next 4; with **MC**, sc in next 11; with **CC**, sc in next 4; with **MC**, sc in next 12, turn.

Row 62: Ch 1, sc in next 12; with **CC**, sc in next 4; with **MC**, sc in next 11; with **CC**, sc in next 4; with **MC**, sc in next 16; with **CC**, sc in next 13; with **MC**, sc in next 23; with **CC**, sc in next 4; with **MC**, sc in next 3; with **CC**, sc in next 4; with **MC**, sc in next 16, turn.

Row 63: Ch 1, sc in next 16; with **CC**, sc in next 4; with **MC**, sc in next 3; with **CC**, sc in next 3; with **MC**, sc in next 25; with **CC**, sc in next 13; with **MC**, sc in next 15; with **CC**, sc in next 4; with **MC**, sc in next 11; with **CC**, sc in next 4; with **MC**, sc in next 12, turn.

Row 64: Ch 1, sc in next 12; with **CC**, sc in next 4; with **MC**, sc in next 11; with **CC**, sc in next 4; with **MC**, sc in next 10; with **CC**, sc in next 2; with **MC**, sc in next 3; with **CC**, sc in next 4; with **MC**, sc in next 34; with **CC**, sc in next 4; with **MC**, sc in next 2; with **CC**, sc in next 3; with **MC**, sc in next 17, turn.

Row 65: Ch 1, sc in next 17; with **CC**, sc in next 4; with **MC**, sc in next; with **CC**, sc in next 4; with **MC**, sc in next 34; with **CC**, sc in next 4; with **MC**, sc in next 3; with **CC**, sc in next 2; with **MC**, sc in next 10; with **CC**, sc in next 4; with **MC**, sc in next 11; with **CC**, sc in next 4; with **MC**, sc in next 12, turn.

Row 66: Ch 1, sc in next 12; with **CC**, sc in next 4; with **MC**, sc in next 11; with **CC**, sc in next 4; with **MC**, sc in next 10; with **CC**, sc in next 2; with **MC**, sc in next 3; with **CC**, sc in next

4; with **MC**, sc in next 34; with **CC**, sc in next 4; with **MC**, sc in next; with **CC**, sc in next 4; with **MC**, sc in next 17, turn.

Row 67: Ch 1, sc in next 18; with **CC**, sc in next 3; with **MC**, sc in next; with **CC**, sc in next 3; with **MC**, sc in next 35; with **CC**, sc in next 4; with **MC**, sc in next 3; with **CC**, sc in next 2; with **MC**, sc in next 10; with **CC**, sc in next 4; with **MC**, sc in next 11; with **CC**, sc in next 4; with **MC**, sc in next 12, turn.

Row 68: Ch 1, sc in next 12; with **CC**, sc in next 4; with **MC**, sc in next 11; with **CC**, sc in next 4; with **MC**, sc in next 11; with **CC**, sc in next 2; with **MC**, sc in next 2; with **CC**, sc in next 4; with **MC**, sc in next 35; with **CC**, sc in next 7; with **MC**, sc in next 18, turn.

Row 69: Ch 1, sc in next 18; with **CC**, sc in next 7; with **MC**, sc in next 24; with **CC**, sc in next 15; with **MC**, sc in next 2; with **CC**, sc in next 2; with **MC**, sc in next 5; with **CC**, sc in next 15; with **MC**, sc in next 6; with **CC**, sc in next 4; with **MC**, sc in next 12, turn.

Row 70: Ch 1, sc in next 12; with **CC**, sc in next 4; with **MC**, sc in next 5; with **CC**, sc in next 17; with **MC**, sc in next 4; with **CC**, sc in next 2; with **MC**, sc in next 3; with **CC**, sc in next 14; with **MC**, sc in next 25; with **CC**, sc in next 5; with **MC**, sc in next 19, turn.

Row 71: Ch 1, sc in next 19; with **CC**, sc in next 5; with **MC**, sc in next 25; with **CC**, sc in next 14; with **MC**, sc in next 3; with **CC**, sc in next 2; with **MC**, sc in next 4; with **CC**, sc in next 17; with **MC**, sc in next 5; with **CC**, sc in next 4; with **MC**, sc in next 12, turn.

Row 72: Ch 1, sc in next 12; with **CC**, sc in next 4; with **MC**, sc in next 5; with **CC**, sc in next 17; with **MC**, sc in next 10; with **CC**, sc in next 13; with **MC**, sc in next 25; with **CC**, sc in next 5; with **MC**, sc in next 19, turn.

Row 73: Ch 1, sc in next 20; with **CC**, sc in next 3; with **MC**, sc in next 27; with **CC**, sc in next 11; with **MC**, sc in next 12; with **CC**, sc in next 16; with **MC**, sc in next 5; with **CC**, sc in next 3; with **MC**, sc in next 13, turn.

Rows 74–76: With **MC**, ch 1, sc in each st across, turn.

Row 77: With **CC**, ch 1, sc in each st across, turn.

Rows 78–79: With **MC**, ch 1, sc in each st across, turn.

Rows 80–81: With **CC**, ch 1, sc in each st across, turn.

Rows 82–83: With **MC**, ch 1, sc in each st across, turn.

Rows 84–85: With **CC**, ch 1, sc in each st across, turn.

Rows 86–89: With **MC**, ch 1, sc in each st across, turn.

Do not fasten off. Proceed to Border.

BORDER

Working around Bath Mat with RS facing.

Rnd 1: 2 sc in same st as last st from Row 89 (place a stitch marker (pm) in first sc), rotate Bath Mat to work in row ends, sc in each row end across, 3 sc in corner (pm in middle st), rotate to work along bottom, sc in each ch across, 3 sc in corner (pm in middle st), rotate to work in row ends, sc in each row end across, 3 sc corner (pm in middle st), rotate to work along top, sc in each st across, join with a sl st in first sc – 402 sts. Do not turn.

Rnd 2: Ch 1, 3 sc in first st, sc in each st around, placing 3 sc in marked st at corners, join with a sl st in first sc – 410 sts.

Fasten off.

FINISHING

Blocking your Bath Mat will allow the carried yarn to settle through the pattern and is a good opportunity to smooth out any minor differences in tension. Wet blocking is recommended, using blocking mats and pins or combs to ensure straight edges. Leave to air dry completely before weaving in all ends on the WS.

CHART

KEY ☐ Main ■ Contrast

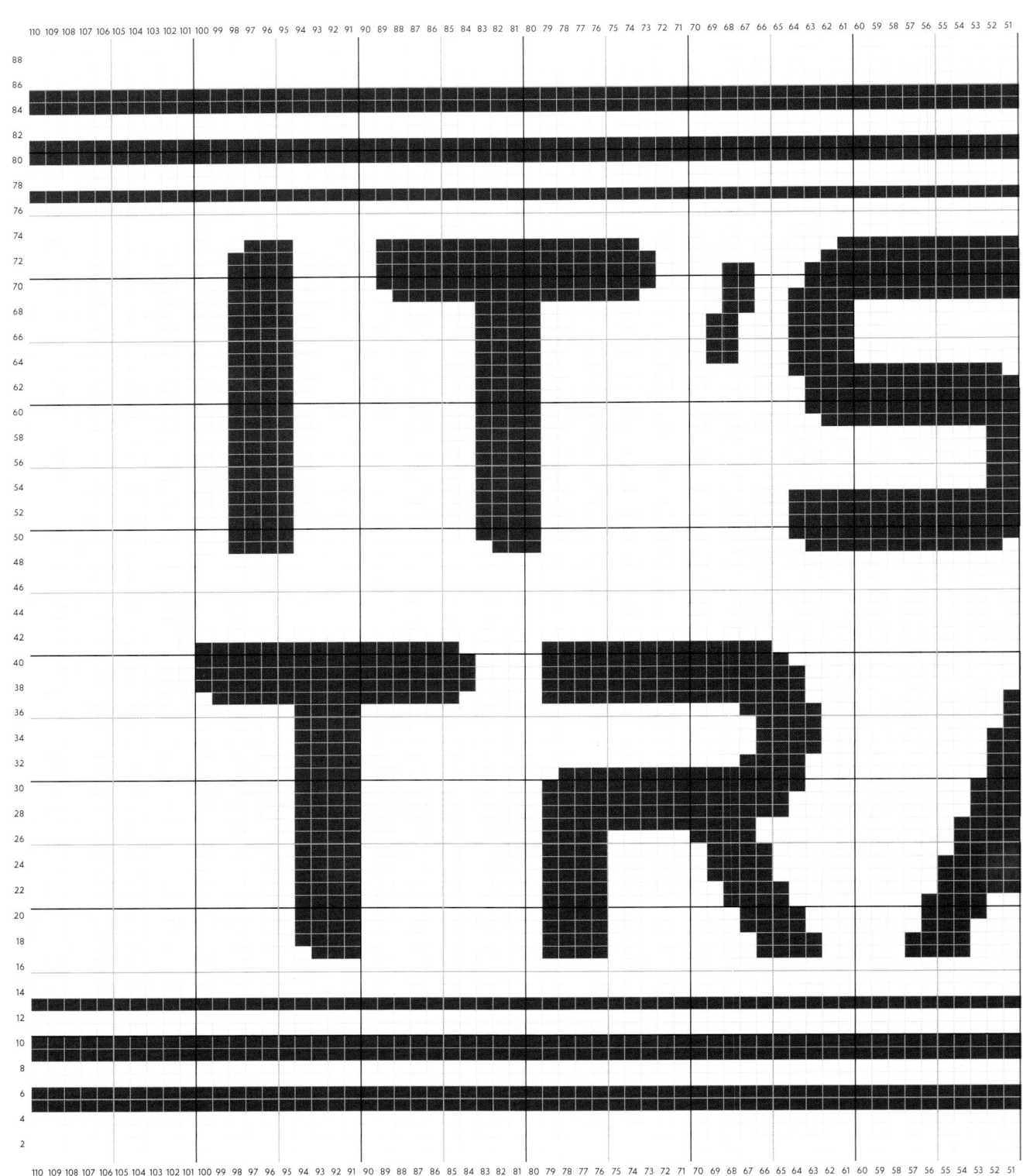

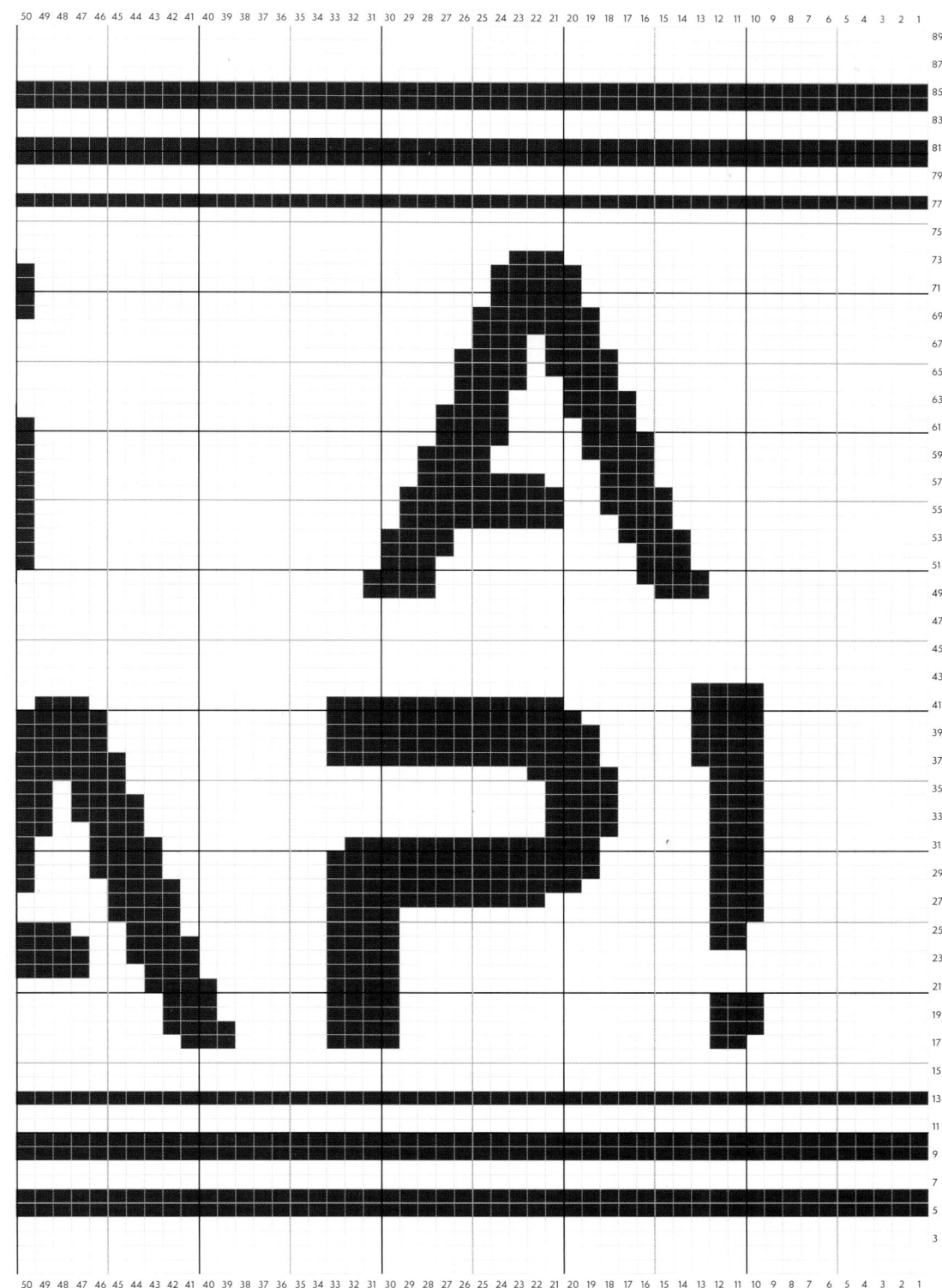

HOME DÉCOR & GIFTS 115

BB-8 TEA COSY

Designed by Leah Parker

SKILL LEVEL: ///

Rolling onto the screen and into hearts over the course of the *Star Wars* sequel trilogy, BB-8 is the newest droid to join in the adventures of the Resistance. This skittish but loyal astromech droid rides along with Resistance pilot Poe Dameron. Flying throughout the galaxy on Poe's X-wing starfighter, these two heroes survive some perilous situations together. When Poe is captured by the First Order on one such mission to Jakku, BB-8 escapes into the desert with a very crucial clue to the location of Luke Skywalker. From there, the droid teams up with Rey and Finn to return the clue to the Resistance base and finish Poe's mission.

A helpful droid can be the difference between winning or losing a battle. Let this BB-8 Tea Cosy help you beat the cold, keeping your tea warm and your teapot adorable in the process. This pattern is designed to slip over the top of a teapot. The dryable, machine-washable yarn makes it practical for everyday use. Colourwork and detailed panels bring this cosy project to life—making it ideal for intermediate crocheters and adventurous beginners willing to see this mission through to the end.

"YOU'RE OKAY. HE'S WITH THE RESISTANCE. HE'S GOING TO GET YOU HOME. WE BOTH WILL."

—Rey, *The Force Awakens*

SIZE
To fit: 6-cup (8-cup) teapot

FINISHED MEASUREMENTS
Height: 7 (8) in. / 18 (20) cm
Bottom width: 11 in. / 28 cm (both sizes)
Sample is shown in 8-cup size.

YARN
Worsted weight (medium #4) shown in Lion Brand Yarn *Vanna's Choice Yarn* (100% Acrylic, 170 yd. / 156 m per 3½ oz. / 100 g ball)
Colour A: #860-100 White, 1 ball
Colour B: #860-149J Silver Grey, 1 ball
Colour C: #860-134A Terracotta, 1 ball
Colour D: #860-153 Black, 1 ball

HOOK
US I-9 / 5.50 mm crochet hook, or *size needed to obtain gauge*

NOTIONS
Tapestry needle
Locking stitch markers
Bobbins (optional)

GAUGE
12 sts and 11 rnds = 4 in. / 10 cm in hdc
Make sure to check your gauge.

PATTERN NOTES
- Drop colour when not in use.
- Each square on the graph represents one hdc. The graph is read from right to left and left to right (*left-handed crocheters will work in the opposite direction*), top to bottom.
- The intarsia colourwork can be worked using bobbins, or carrying the yarn, or a combination of both.

HOME DÉCOR & GIFTS

COSY

Rnd 1: With **A**, 12 hdc in a magic ring, join with sl st in first st – 12 sts.

Rnd 2: Ch 1, 2 hdc in each st around, join with sl st in first st – 24 sts.

Rnd 3: Ch 1, [2 hdc in next st, hdc in next] around, join with sl st in first st – 36 sts.

Rnd 4: With **B**, ch 1, [2 hdc in next st, hdc in next 2] around, join with sl st in first st – 48 sts.

Rnd 5: Ch 1, [2 hdc in next st, hdc in next 3] around, join with sl st in first st – 60 sts.

Rnd 6: With **A**, ch 1, hdc in each st around, join with sl st in first st.

Rnd 7: With **C**, ch 1, hdc in next 10 sts; with **A**, hdc in next 10 sts; with **C**, hdc in next 40 sts, join with sl st in first st – 60 sts.

SPLIT FOR FRONT PANEL

Working in rows:

Row 8: With **A**, ch 1, hdc in next 30 sts.

Rows 9–15: Turn, ch 1, hdc in each st across.

Row 16: Turn, with **C**, ch 1, hdc in next 5 sts; with **A**, hdc in next 2 sts; with **C**, hdc in next 2 sts; with **A**, hdc in next 16 sts; with **C**, hdc in next 5 sts – 30 sts.

Row 17: Turn, with **C**, ch 1, hdc in next 5 sts; with **A**, hdc in next 2 sts; with **C**, hdc in next 2 sts; with **A**, hdc in next 12 sts; with **C**, hdc in next 2 sts; with **A**, hdc in next 2 sts with **C**, hdc in next 5 sts – 30 sts.

Row 18: Turn, with **B**, ch 1, hdc in each st across – 30 sts.

Fasten off.

BACK PANEL

Row 8 continued: With RS facing, join **A** to first unworked st after Front Panel, ch 1, hdc in next 30 sts.

Rows 9–15: Turn, ch 1, hdc in each st across.

Row 16: Turn, with **A**, ch 1, hdc in next 2 sts; with **C**, hdc in next 2; with **A**, hdc in next 2; with **C**, hdc in next 2; with **A**, hdc in next 2; with **C**, hdc in next 5; with **A**, hdc in next; with **C**, hdc in next 2; with **A**, hdc in next; with **C**, hdc in next 5; with **A**, hdc in next 2; with **C**, hdc in next 2; with **A**, hdc in next 2 – 30 sts.

Row 17: Turn, with **A**, ch 1, hdc in next 2 sts; with **C**, hdc in next 2; with **A**, hdc in next 2; with **C**, hdc in next 5; with **A**, hdc in next; with **C**, hdc in next 2; with **A**, hdc in next; with **C**, hdc in next 5; with **A**, hdc in next 2; with **C**, hdc in next 2; with **A**, hdc in next 2; with **C**, hdc in next 2; with **A**, hdc in next 2 – 30 sts.

Row 18: Turn, with **B**, ch 1, hdc in each st across.

Do not fasten off.

CLOSE BOTTOM OF COSY

Working in rnds.

Rnd 19: Ch 1, hdc in each st around Front Panel and Back Panel, join with sl st in first st – 60 sts. *End here for the 6-cup Cosy.*

Rnds 20–21: Ch 1, hdc in each st around, join with sl st in first st.

Fasten off.

SENSOR DETAIL 1

Rnd 1: With **D**, 6 hdc in a magic ring, join with sl st in first st – 6 sts.

Rnd 2: Ch 1, 2 hdc in each st around, join with sl st in first st – 12 sts.

Rnd 3: Ch 1, [2 hdc in next st, hdc in next] around, join with sl st in first st – 18 sts.

Fasten off, leaving a long tail to sew detail onto Cosy.

Position evenly between Colour **C** sections on Round 7. Pin in place and sew onto Cosy.

SENSOR DETAIL 2

Rnd 1: With **D**, 6 hdc in a magic ring, join with sl st in first st – 6 sts.

Rnd 2: With **A**, ch 1, 2 sc in each st around, join with sl st in first st – 12 sts.

Rnd 3: With **D**, ch 1, [2 sc in next st, sc in next] around, join with sl st in first st – 18 sts.

Fasten off, leaving a long tail to sew detail onto Cosy.

Position to the right of Sensor Detail 1, just above the small Colour **C** marking on Row 17. Pin in place and sew onto Cosy.

SENSOR DETAIL 3

Rnd 1: With **B**, 6 hdc in a magic ring, join with sl st in first st – 6 sts.

Fasten off, leaving a long tail to sew detail onto Cosy.

Centre below Sensor Detail 1. Pin in place and sew onto Cosy.

FINISHING

Join **A** anywhere around handle opening.

Rnd 1: Sc evenly around opening, join with sl st in first st. Fasten off.

Repeat around spout opening.

Weave in ends.

CHART

KEY A B C

FRONT

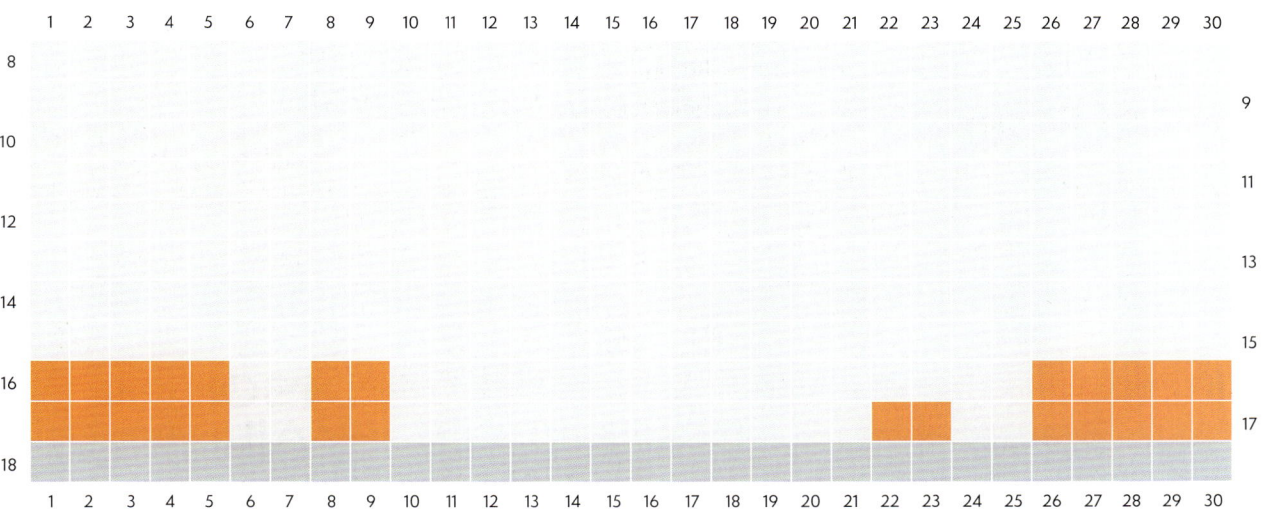

BACK

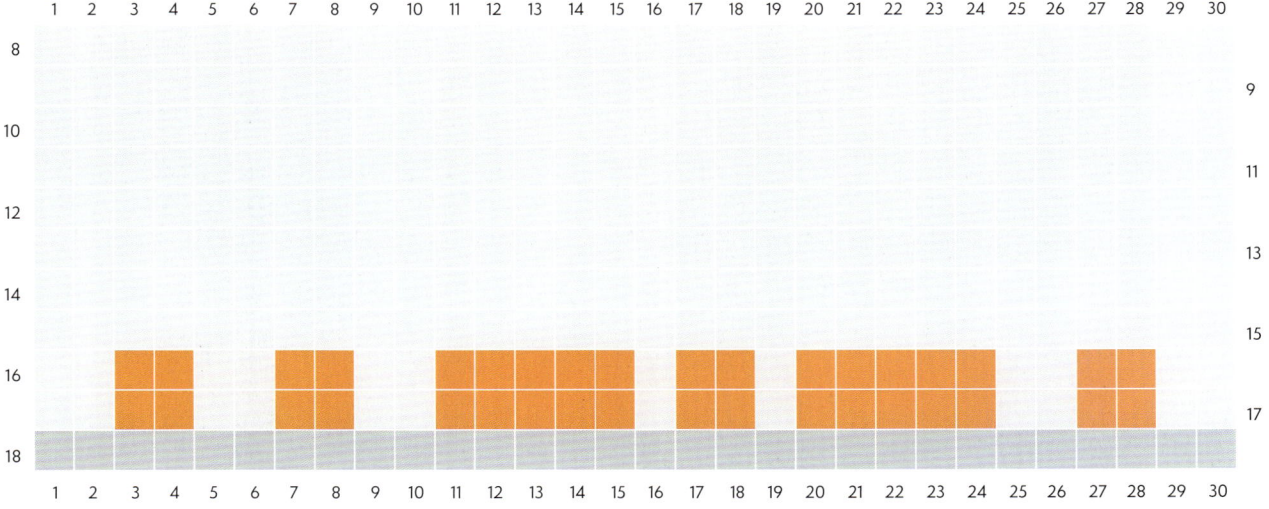

HOME DÉCOR & GIFTS 119

IMPERIAL TRIVET

Designed by Leah Parker

SKILL LEVEL: ✦✦✦

The Galactic Empire, an autocracy ruled by Emperor Palpatine, replaces the Galactic Republic at the end of the Clone Wars. During this time, former senator of Naboo and Supreme Chancellor Palpatine rises to power by promising to bring order to the galaxy. However, his regime operates on fear, intimidation, and oppression. Eventually, audiences learn that Palpatine leads a double life as a Sith Lord called Darth Sidious. His goal is to destroy the Jedi Order. His authority, and the Empire itself, may seem indestructible, but like the Empire's famous planet-destroying Death Star, there are vulnerabilities in Emperor Palpatine's plans. Smaller rebel groups prove as much, when they unite to form the Rebel Alliance and hatch their own plan to destroy the Death Star.

Like the Galactic Empire at the height of its power, this trivet relies on strength and order, making use of a durable cotton yarn to withstand warm temperatures. Utilizing crochet colourwork while working in the round, this pattern showcases the bold, geometric features of the Imperial insignia. It's for those looking to try out colourwork on a simple yet functional project. Whether you are a rebel in the kitchen or prefer to cook with Imperial precision, this trivet will stand strong through culinary challenges.

SIZE
One size

FINISHED MEASUREMENTS
Diameter: approximately 9.5 in. / 24 cm

YARN
Worsted weight (medium #4) shown in Lion Brand Yarn *24/7 Cotton* (100% Cotton, 186 yd. / 170 m per 3½ oz. / 100 g ball)
Colour A: White, 1 ball
Colour B: Black, 1 ball

HOOK
US F-5 / 3.75 mm crochet hook, or *size needed to obtain gauge*

NOTIONS
Tapestry needle
Locking stitch markers

GAUGE
24 sts and 11 rnds = 4 in. / 10 cm in hdc
Make sure to check your gauge.

PATTERN NOTES
- Starting ch-2 does not count as a stitch.
- When changing colours, crochet as normal but on the hdc before the colour change, work the hdc until you have 3 loops on your hook and then pull in the new colour to finish the stitch. Continue working with the new colour.
- Work over colour not in use.

"EVERYTHING THAT HAS TRANSPIRED HAS DONE SO ACCORDING TO MY DESIGN."

—Emperor Palpatine,
Return of the Jedi

PATTERN

Rnd 1: With **A**, 12 hdc in a magic ring, join with sl st in first hdc – 12 sts.

Rnd 2: Ch 2, 2 hdc in each st around, join with sl st in first hdc – 24 sts.

Rnd 3: Ch 2, *2 hdc in first st, hdc in next, rep from * around, join with sl st in first hdc – 36 sts.

Rnd 4: Ch 2, *with **A**, 2 hdc in first st, hdc in next 2; with **B**, 2 hdc in next, hdc in next 2, rep from * around; with **A**, join with sl st in first hdc – 48 sts.

Rnd 5: Ch 2, *with **A**, 2 hdc in first st, hdc in next 3; with **B**, 2 hdc in next, hdc in next 3, rep from * around; with **A**, join with sl st in first hdc – 60 sts.

Rnd 6: Ch 2, *with **A**, 2 hdc in first st, hdc in next 4; with **B**, 2 hdc in next, hdc in next 4, rep from * around; with **A**, join with sl st in first hdc – 72 sts.

Rnd 7: Ch 2, *with **A**, 2 hdc in first st, hdc in next 5; with **B**, 2 hdc in next, hdc in next 5, rep from * around; with **A**, join with sl st in first hdc – 84 sts.

Rnd 8: Ch 2, *with **A**, 2 hdc in first st, hdc in next 6; with **B**, 2 hdc in next, hdc in next 6, rep from * around, join with a sl st in first hdc – 96 sts.

Rnd 9: Ch 2, *2 hdc in first st, hdc in next 7, rep from * around, join with sl st in first hdc – 108 sts.

Rnd 10: Ch 2, *2 hdc in first st, hdc in next 8; with **A**, 2 hdc in next, hdc in next 8, rep from * around, join with sl st in first hdc – 120 sts.

Rnd 11: Ch 2, *2 hdc in first st, hdc in next 2; with **B**, hdc in next 4; with **A**, hdc in next 3, 2 hdc in next, hdc in next 9, rep from * around; with **B**, join with sl st in first hdc – 132 sts.

Rnd 12: Ch 2, *2 hdc in first st, hdc in next 10, rep from * around, join with sl st in first hdc – 144 sts.

Fasten off and weave in ends.

Block to finished measurements.

"YOUR FEEBLE SKILLS ARE NO MATCH FOR THE POWER OF THE DARK SIDE."

—Emperor Palpatine, *Star Wars:* Episode VI—*Return of the Jedi*

TATOOINE LANDSCAPE BLANKET

Designed by Leah Parker

SKILL LEVEL: ✎ ✎ ✎ ✎

Tatooine is an unforgiving desert planet with twin scorching suns, located in the galaxy's Outer Rim. Due to the relentless heat, there isn't always sufficient water to support its population, leading many inhabitants to turn to moisture farming. They extract what water they can from the atmosphere. These harsh conditions push some to lawlessness. In the final years of the Republic, Tatooine is controlled by the Hutts, and subject to their criminal empire.

There's more to Tatooine than heat and crime. Powerful Jedi Knights Luke and Anakin Skywalker both spent formative years on the desert planet. And, during the Galactic Civil War, Tatooine catches the attention of the Empire when an escape pod carrying stolen Death Star plans, along with the droids C-3PO and R2-D2, crash-lands on its sandy surface.

A far away planet with a big role in the *Star Wars* films, Tatooine is the inspiration for this cosy blanket pattern in more ways than one. This blanket is worked flat back and forth in rows, capturing the planet's vast desert and twin suns through the use of the tapestry crochet technique. While the project's design evokes this iconic landscape, the process of crafting it may require resilience and determination—qualities Tatooine's inhabitants are shown to have in spades. So, as you crochet your way around Tatooine's two suns, remember: They may be a source of blistering heat, but they also produce breathtaking sunsets.

"IF THERE'S A BRIGHT CENTRE TO THE UNIVERSE, YOU'RE ON THE PLANET IT'S FARTHEST FROM."

—Luke Skywalker on Tatooine, *A New Hope*

SIZE
One size

FINISHED MEASUREMENTS
Length: 36½ in. / 93 cm
Width: 48 in / 122 cm

YARN
Worsted weight (medium #4) shown in Lion Brand Yarn *Pound of Love* (100% Acrylic, 1020 yd. / 932 m per 16 oz. / 454 g ball)
Colour A: #550-149 Charcoal, 1 ball
Colour B: #550-135N Pumpkin Pie, 1 ball
Colour C: #550-104Q Pink Salt, 1 ball
Colour D: #550-158M Honey Bee, 1 ball
Colour E: #550-141R Quartz, 1 ball
Colour F: #550-145T Thistle, 1 ball

HOOK
US J-10 / 6.00 mm crochet hook, or *size needed to obtain gauge*

NOTIONS
Tapestry needle
Locking stitch markers

GAUGE
11 sts and 11 rows = 4 in. / 10 cm in hdc
Make sure to check your gauge.

PATTERN NOTES
- When changing colours, drop colour not in use to the back of the work.
- Where there are only a few stitches between colour changes, work over the colour not in use. If there are larger spaces between colour changes, it is recommended to cut the unused colour and join as needed.
- The graph shows 1 hdc per square and is worked from the bottom up.
- Odd-number rows are on the RS, worked from right to left on the chart. Even-number rows are on the WS, worked from left to right on the chart. Left-handed crocheters work in reverse: RS from left to right and WS from right to left.
- Carry yarn on the WS.

HOME DÉCOR & GIFTS

PATTERN

To follow the graph:

With **A**, ch 102, then follow the graph from the bottom up.

Row 1 (RS): With **A**, ch 102, hdc in third ch from hook and in each ch across – 100 sts.

Rows 2–22: Ch 1, turn, hdc in each st across.

Row 23: Ch 1, turn, with **B**, hdc in next 15; with **A**, hdc in next 7; with **B**, hdc in next 4; with **A**, hdc in next 10; with **B**, hdc in next 19; with **A**, hdc in next 32; with **B**, hdc in next 13.

Row 24: Ch 1, turn, with **B**, hdc in next 13; with **A**, hdc in next 32; with **B**, hdc in next 19; with **A**, hdc in next 10; with **B**, hdc in next 4; with **A**, hdc in next 7; with **B**, hdc in next 15.

Row 25: Ch 1, turn, with **B**, hdc in next 26; with **A**, hdc in next 10; with **B**, hdc in next 19; with **A**, hdc in next 32; with **B**, hdc in next 13.

Row 26: Ch 1, turn, with **B**, hdc in next 13; with **A**, hdc in next 32; with **B**, hdc in next 55.

Row 27: Ch 1, turn, with **B**, hdc in next 55; with **A**, hdc in next 32; with **B**, hdc in next 13.

Row 28: Ch 1, turn, with **B**, hdc in next 13; with **A**, hdc in next 32; with **B**, hdc in next 55.

Row 29: Ch 1, turn, with **B**, hdc in next 55; with **A**, hdc in next 32; with **B**, hdc in next 13.

Row 30: Ch 1, turn, with **B**, hdc in next 14; with **A**, hdc in next 29; with **B**, hdc in next 57.

Row 31: Ch 1, turn, with **C**, hdc in next 2; with **B**, hdc in next 56; with **A**, hdc in next 27; with **B**, hdc in next 15.

Row 32: Ch 1, turn, with **B**, hdc in next 15; with **A**, hdc in next 26; with **B**, hdc in next 53; with **C**, hdc in next 6.

Row 33: Ch 1, turn, with **C**, hdc in next 8; with **B**, hdc in next 52; with **A**, hdc in next 24; with **B**, hdc in next 16.

Row 34: Ch 1, turn, with **B**, hdc in next 16; with **A**, hdc in next 20; with **B**, hdc in next 51; with **C**, hdc in next 13.

Row 35: Ch 1, turn, with **C**, hdc in next 22; with **B**, hdc in next 43; with **A**, hdc in next 18; with **B**, hdc in next 17.

Row 36: Ch 1, turn, with **B**, hdc in next 18; with **A**, hdc in next 16; with **B**, hdc in next 37; with **C**, hdc in next 29.

BEHIND THE SCENES

Many of the scenes set on Tatooine, in *A New Hope*, were filmed in the deserts of Tunisia.

Row 37: Ch 1, turn, with **C**, hdc in next 37; with **B**, hdc in next 31; with **A**, hdc in next 13; with **B**, hdc in next 19.

Row 38: Ch 1, turn, with **B**, hdc in next 21; with **A**, hdc in next 10; with **B**, hdc in next 24; with **C**, hdc in next 45.

Row 39: Ch 1, turn, with **C**, hdc in next 51; with **B**, hdc in next 21; with **A**, hdc in next 4; with **B**, hdc in next 24.

Fasten off **A**.

Row 40: Ch 1, turn, with **B**, hdc in next 42; with **C**, hdc in next 58.

Row 41: Ch 1, turn, with **C**, hdc in next 61; with **B**, hdc in next 39.

Row 42: Ch 1, turn, with **B**, hdc in next 37; with **C**, hdc in next 63.

Row 43: Ch 1, turn, with **C**, hdc in next 65; with **B**, hdc in next 35.

Row 44: Ch 1, turn, with **B**, hdc in next 33; with **C**, hdc in next 67.

Row 45: Ch 1, turn, with **C**, hdc in next 68; with **B**, hdc in next 32.

Row 46: Ch 1, turn, with **B**, hdc in next 27; with **C**, hdc in next 40; with **D**, hdc in next 9; with **C**, hdc in next 24.

Row 47: Ch 1, turn, with **C**, hdc in next 22; with **D**, hdc in next 13; with **C**, hdc in next 42; with **B**, hdc in next 23.

Row 48: Ch 1, turn, with **B**, hdc in next 20; with **C**, hdc in next 45; with **D**, hdc in next 15; with **C**, hdc in next 20.

Row 49: Ch 1, turn, with **C**, hdc in next 19; with **D**, hdc in next 17; with **C**, hdc in next 53; with **B**, hdc in next 11.

Row 50: Ch 1, turn, with **B**, hdc in next 9 hdc; with **C**, hdc in next 54; with **D**, hdc in next 19; with **C**, hdc in next 18.

Row 51: Ch 1, turn, with **C**, hdc in next 17; with **D**, hdc in next 20; with **C**, hdc in next 58; with **B**, hdc in next 5.

Row 52: Ch 1, turn, with **B**, hdc in next 3; with **C**, hdc in next 59; with **D**, hdc in next 21; with **C**, hdc in next 17.

Row 53: Ch 1, turn, with **C**, hdc in next 16; with **D**, hdc in next 22; with **C**, hdc in next 61; with **B**, hdc in next.

Fasten off **B**.

Row 54: Ch 1, turn, with **C**, hdc in next 61; with **D**, hdc in next 23; with **C**, hdc in next 16.

Row 55: Ch 1, turn, with **C**, hdc in next 16; with **D**, hdc in next 23; with **C**, hdc in next 61.

Row 56: Ch 1, turn, with **C**, hdc in next 61; with **D**, hdc in next 23; with **C**, hdc in next 16.

Row 57: Ch 1, turn, with **C**, hdc in next 16; with **D**, hdc in next 23; with **C**, hdc in next 61.

Row 58: Ch 1, turn, with **C**, hdc in next 61; with **D**, hdc in next 23; with **C**, hdc in next 16.

Row 59: Ch 1, turn, with **C**, hdc in next 16; with **D**, hdc in next 23; with **C**, hdc in next 34; with **E**, hdc in next 11; with **C**, hdc in next 16.

Row 60: Ch 1, turn, with **C**, hdc in next 14; with **E**, hdc in next 20; with **C**, hdc in next 27; with **D**, hdc in next 23; with **C**, hdc in next 16.

Row 61: Ch 1, turn, with **C**, hdc in next

16; with **D**, hdc in next 23; with **C**, hdc in next 22; with **E**, hdc in next 31; with **C**, hdc in next 8.

Row 62: Ch 1, turn, with **C**, hdc in next 5; with **E**, hdc in next 45; with **C**, hdc in next 12; with **D**, hdc in next 22; with **C**, hdc in next 16.

Row 63: Ch 1, turn, with **C**, hdc in next 17; with **D**, hdc in next 20; with **C**, hdc in next 9; with **E**, hdc in next 51; with **C**, hdc in next 3.

Row 64: Ch 1, turn, with **E**, hdc in next 59; with **C**, hdc in next 4 hdc; with **D**, hdc in next 19 hdc; with **C**, hdc in next 18.

Row 65: Ch 1, turn, with **C**, hdc in next 19; with **D**, hdc in next 17; with **C**, hdc in next 2; with **E**, hdc in next 62.

Row 66: Ch 1, turn, with **E**, hdc in next 65; with **D**, hdc in next 15; with **C**, hdc in next 20.

Row 67: Ch 1, turn, with **C**, hdc in next 21; with **D**, hdc in next 13; with **E**, hdc in next 66.

Row 68: Ch 1, turn, with **E**, hdc in next 67; with **D**, hdc in next 11; with **C**, hdc in next 22.

Row 69: Ch 1, turn, with **C**, hdc in next 17; with **E**, hdc in next 6; with **D**, hdc in next 8; with **E**, hdc in next 69.

Row 70: Ch 1, turn, with **E**, hdc in next 86; with **C**, hdc in next 14.

Row 71: Ch 1, turn, with **C**, hdc in next 10; with **E**, hdc in next 90.

Row 72: Ch 1, turn, with **E**, hdc in next 92; with **C**, hdc in next 8.

Row 73: Ch 1, turn, with **C**, hdc in next 6; with **E**, hdc in next 94.

Row 74: Ch 1, turn, with **E**, hdc in next 96; with **C**, hdc in next 4.

Row 75: Ch 1, turn, with **C**, hdc in next 2; with **E**, hdc in next 98.

Row 76: Ch 1, turn, with **F**, hdc in next 3; with **E**, hdc in next 96; with **C**, hdc in next.

Fasten off **C**.

Row 77: Ch 1, turn, with **E**, hdc in next 95; with **F**, hdc in next 5.

Row 78: Ch 1, turn, with **F**, hdc in next 9; with **E**, hdc in next 91.

Row 79: Ch 1, turn, with **E**, hdc in next 86; with **F**, hdc in next 14.

Row 80: Ch 1, turn, with **F**, hdc in next 19; with **E**, hdc in next 81.

Row 81: Ch 1, turn, with **E**, hdc in next 77; with **F**, hdc in next 23.

Row 82: Ch 1, turn, with **F**, hdc in next 29; with **E**, hdc in next 71.

Row 83: Ch 1, turn, with **E**, hdc in next 70; with **F**, hdc in next 30.

Row 84: Ch 1, turn, with **F**, hdc in next 32; with **E**, hdc in next 68.

Row 85: Ch 1, turn, with **E**, hdc in next 65; with **F**, hdc in next 35.

Row 86: Ch 1, turn, with **F**, hdc in next 41; with **E**, hdc in next 59.

Row 87: Ch 1, turn, with **E**, hdc in next 57; with **F**, hdc in next 43.

Row 88: Ch 1, turn, with **F**, hdc in next 44; with **E**, hdc in next 56.

Row 89: Ch 1, turn, with **E**, hdc in next 55; with **F**, hdc in next 45.

Row 90: Ch 1, turn, with **F**, hdc in next 49; with **E**, hdc in next 51.

Row 91: Ch 1, turn, with **E**, hdc in next 49; with **F**, hdc in next 14; with **D**, hdc in next 7; with **F**, hdc in next 30.

Row 92: Ch 1, turn, with **F**, hdc in next 28; with **D**, hdc in next 11; with **F**, hdc in next 14; with **E**, hdc in next 47.

Row 93: Ch 1, turn, with **E**, hdc in next 45; with **F**, hdc in next 15; with **D**, hdc in next 14; with **F**, hdc in next 26.

Row 94: Ch 1, turn, with **F**, hdc in next 26; with **D**, hdc in next 14; with **F**, hdc in next 18; with **E**, hdc in next 42.

Row 95: Ch 1, turn, with **E**, hdc in next 40; with **F**, hdc in next 19; with **D**, hdc in next 16; with **F**, hdc in next 25.

Row 96: Ch 1, turn, with **F**, hdc in next 24; with **D**, hdc in next 18; with **F**, hdc in next 21; with **E**, hdc in next 37.

Row 97: Ch 1, turn, with **E**, hdc in next 36; with **F**, hdc in next 22; with **D**, hdc in next 18; with **F**, hdc in next 24.

Row 98: Ch 1, turn, with **F**, hdc in next 24; with **D**, hdc in next 18; with **F**, hdc in next 25; with **E**, hdc in next 33.

Row 99: Ch 1, turn, with **E**, hdc in next 22; with **F**, hdc in next 36; with **D**, hdc in next 18; with **F**, hdc in next 24.

Row 100: Ch 1, turn, with **F**, hdc in next 24; with **D**, hdc in next 18; with **F**, hdc in next 42; with **E**, hdc in next 16.

Row 101: Ch 1, turn, with **E**, hdc in next 13; with **F**, hdc in next 46; with **D**, hdc in next 17; with **F**, hdc in next 24.

Row 102: Ch 1, turn, with **F**, hdc in next 25; with **D**, hdc in next 16; with **F**, hdc in next 48; with **E**, hdc in next 11.

Row 103: Ch 1, turn, with **E**, hdc in next 7; with **F**, hdc in next 53; with **D**, hdc in next 15; with **F**, hdc in next 25.

Row 104: Ch 1, turn, with **F**, hdc in next 26; with **D**, hdc in next 14; with **F**, hdc in next 58; with **E**, hdc in next 2.

Fasten off **E**.

Row 105: Ch 1, turn, with **F**, hdc in next 61; with **D**, hdc in next 12; with **F**, hdc in next 27.

Row 106: Ch 1, turn, with **F**, hdc in next 28; with **D**, hdc in next 9; with **F**, hdc in next 63.

Row 107: Ch 1, turn, with **F**, hdc in next 65; with **D**, hdc in next 5; with **F**, hdc in next 30.

Fasten off **D**.

Rows 108–132: Ch 1, turn, hdc in each st across.

Fasten off and weave in ends.

CHART

KEY

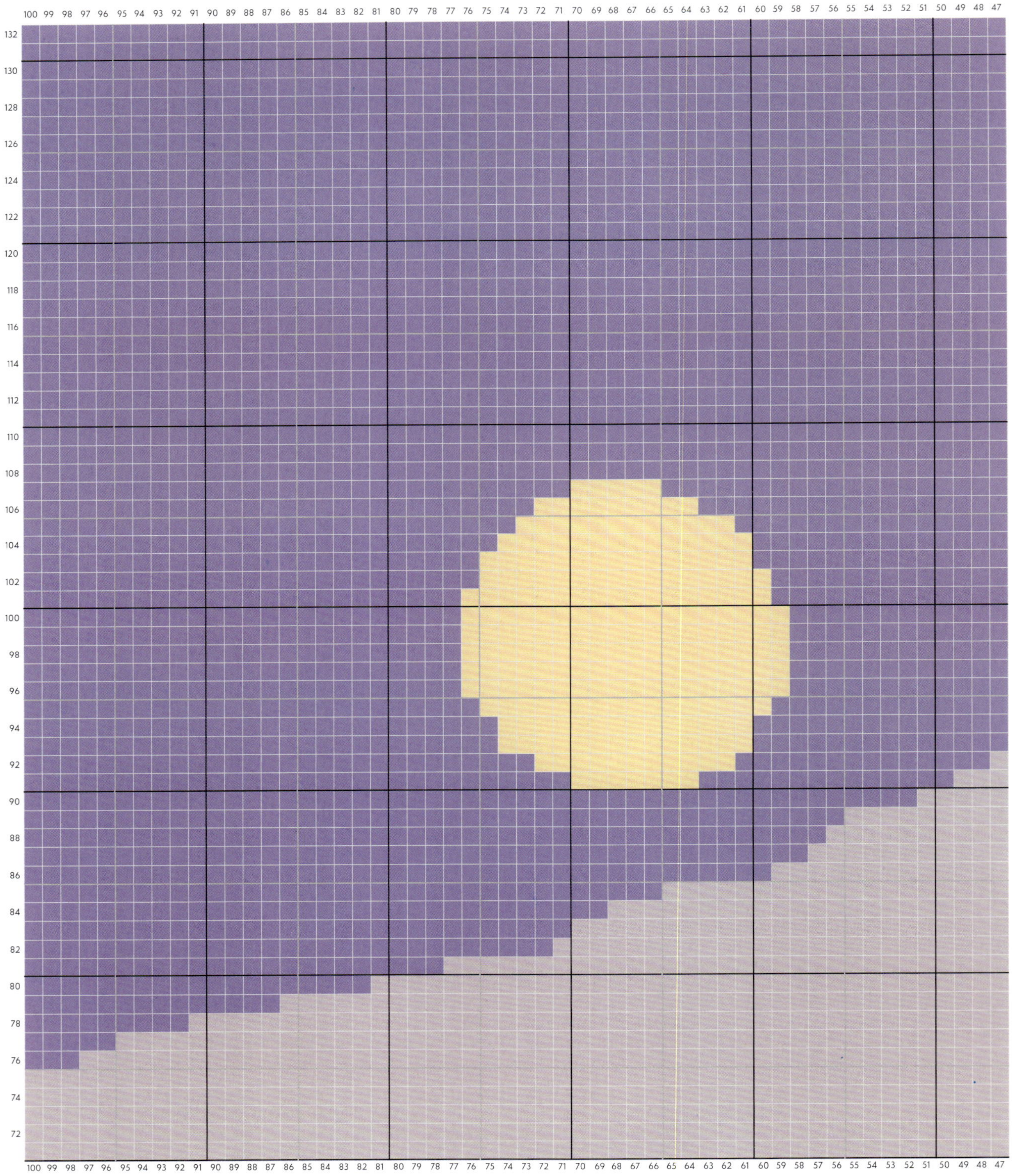

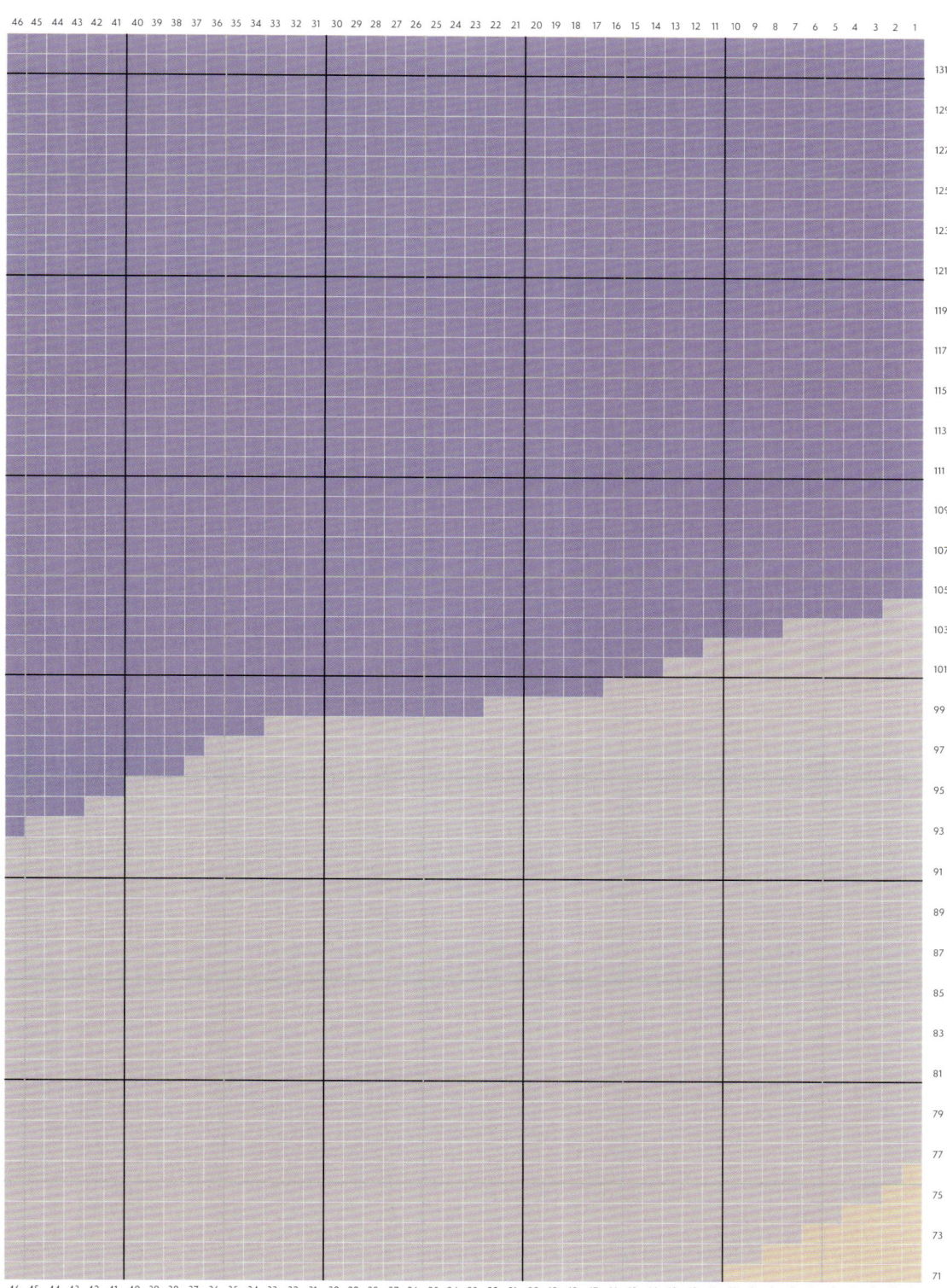

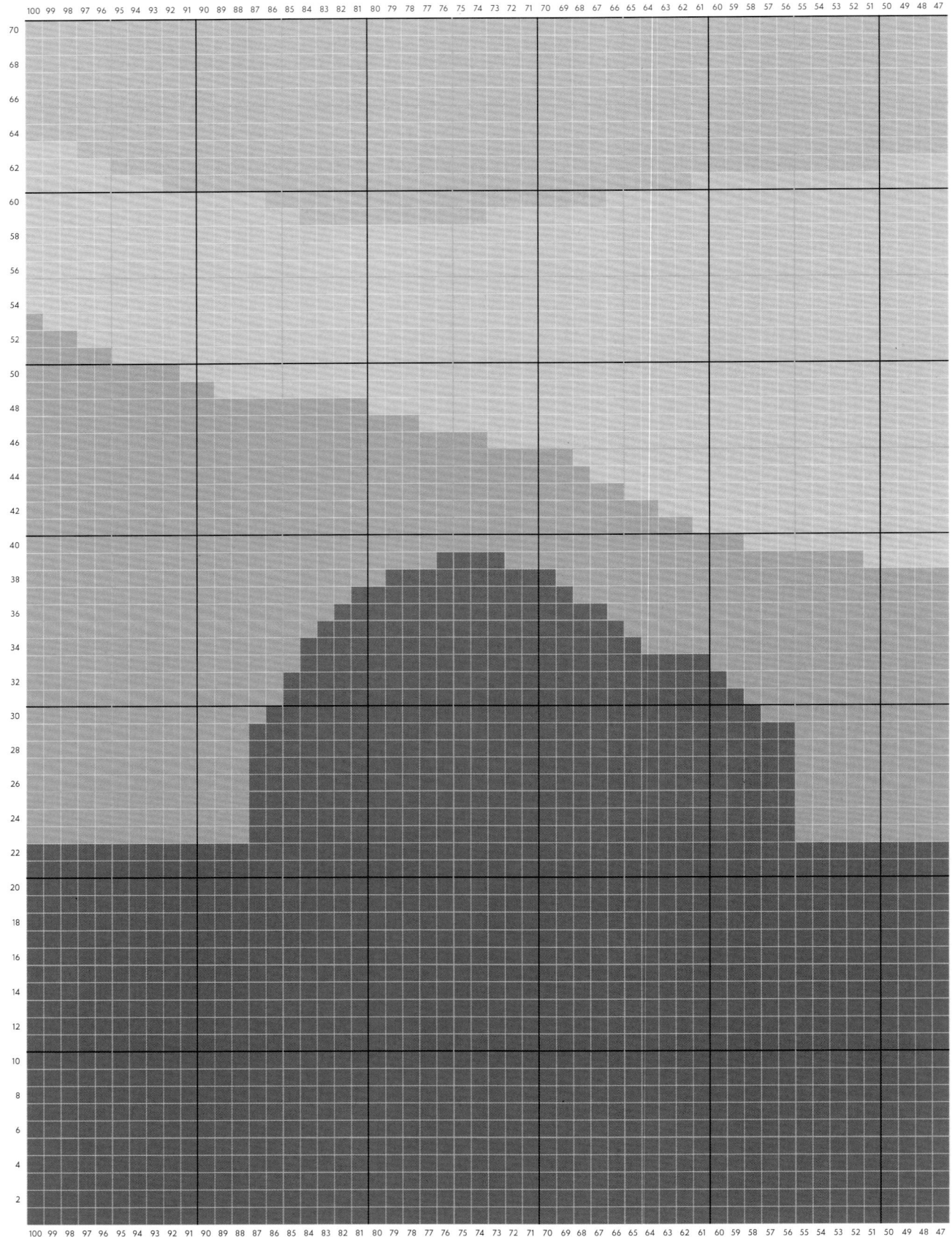

YODA COASTER

Designed by Leah Parker

SKILL LEVEL: ✎

First introduced in *The Empire Strikes Back,* Yoda is a Jedi Master. Revered not just for his skill with the Force, but for his wisdom, Yoda is known for teaching generations of Jedi. Aspiring Jedi Luke Skywalker finds Yoda on the swamp planet Dagobah and begins his own training there. When Luke's X-wing sinks into the swamp and is seemingly lost, Yoda encourages him to raise it using the Force. Luke hesitates, saying, "Moving stones around is one thing. This is totally different." Yoda challenges back, "No! No different. Only different in your mind." To prove the point, he raises Luke's ship from the swampy bog himself.

There's much to think about and unpack when it comes to Yoda's sage advice and iconic quotes. To spark a conversation about it, consider testing out this charming coaster shaped like the Jedi Master. For this pattern, Yoda's head is worked in rounds, while his ears are worked back and forth in rows. Made as three individual pieces and then seamed together, it's a project where the bigger picture reveals itself in stages. If you want to take this project even further, check out the instructions for turning this pattern into an entire garland. The coaster's cotton yarn will protect your surfaces from destruction, like a guardian of peace and balance for your home.

> "DO. OR DO NOT.
> THERE IS NO TRY."
>
> —Yoda, *The Empire Strikes Back*

SIZE
One size

FINISHED MEASUREMENTS
Diameter (Head only): 5 in. / 13 cm
Diameter (with Ears): 11 in. / 28 cm

YARN
Worsted weight (medium #4) shown in Paintbox Yarns *Cotton Aran* (100% Cotton, 93 yd. / 85 m per 1.7 oz. / 50 g ball): 1 ball in #626 Spearmint Green.

HOOK
US G-7 / 4.5 mm crochet hook, or *size needed to obtain gauge*

NOTIONS
Tapestry needle
Locking stitch markers

GAUGE
12 sts and 12 rows = 4 in. / 10 cm in hdc
Make sure to check your gauge.

PATTERN NOTES
- This Coaster can be turned into a Garland! Crochet multiple Coasters and join with a string on the WS at the Ears!
- The Head is worked in rounds, while the Ears are worked back and forth in rows. The three pieces are then assembled to create your very own Yoda Coaster.

SPECIAL ABBREVIATIONS
- **Hdc2tog (half double crochet two together):** Yarn over, insert hook into next stitch and pull up a loop, yarn over, insert hook into next stitch and pull up a loop, yarn over and draw yarn through 5 loops on hook.

EARS (MAKE 2)

Row 1: Ch 12, hdc in third ch and in each ch across, turn – 10 sts.

Rows 2–3: Ch 1, hdc in each st across, turn – 10 sts.

Rows 4–12: Ch 1, hdc2tog, hdc in each st across, turn – 1 st remains after last row.

Fasten off, leaving a long tail for sewing.

HEAD

Rnd 1: 8 hdc in a magic ring, join with sl st in first st – 8 sts.

Rnd 2: Ch 1, 2 hdc in each st around, join with sl st in first st – 16 hdc.

Rnd 3: Ch 1, [2 hdc in next st, hdc in next] around, join with sl st in first st – 24 sts.

Rnd 4: Ch 1, [2 hdc in next st, hdc in next 2] around, join with sl st in first st – 32 sts.

Rnd 5: Ch 1, [2 hdc in next st, hdc in next 3] around, join with sl st in first st – 40 sts.

Rnd 6: Ch 1, [2 hdc in next st, hdc in next 4] around, join with sl st in first st – 48 sts.

Rnd 7: Ch 1, [2 hdc in next st, hdc in next 5] around, join with sl st in first st – 56 sts.

Fasten off and weave in ends.

ASSEMBLY

Fold the Ear on long side at approximately one third of the length.

Place the folded side behind the Head and attach with long tail.

Repeat for the second Ear, leaving approximately 14 stitches between the Ears at the top of the Head.

Weave in ends.

ABBREVIATIONS

beg: begin(ning)
blo: back loop only
bob: 4-hdc bobble stitch
cc: contrast colour
ch: chain
ch sp: chain space
dc: double crochet
dec: decrease
fsc: foundation single crochet
fhdc: foundation half double crochet
hdc: half double crochet
hdc2tog: half double crochet 2 stitches together
inc: increase
inv dec: invisible decrease

mc: main colour
pm: place marker
rem: remain(ing)
rep: repeat
rnd(s): round(s)
RS: right side
sc: single crochet
sc2tog: single crochet 2 stitches together
sk: skip
sl st: slip stitch
st(s): stitch(es)
WS: wrong side
yo: yarn over

YARN RESOURCE GUIDE

ALLISON BARNES YARN: allisonbarnesyarn.com

ANCIENT ARTS YARN: ancientartsfibre.com

BERNAT: yarnspirations.com

HOBBII: hobbii.com

LION BRAND YARN: lionbrand.com

MACE OF SKEINS: maceofskeins.com

MADELINETOSH: madelinetosh.com

PAINTBOX YARNS: paintboxyarns.com

ACKNOWLEDGMENTS

Thank you to Sammy Holland, who took a chance on me and helped get this book off the ground. Your support and belief in this project and me have meant the world to me! Thank you to Alexis Sattler, the best editor on this side of the galaxy! This book would not be what it is without your guidance, sharp eye, and boundless creativity.

I could have not finished this book without my incredible team of designers: Alexis, Janine, Kate, and Romina. Each one of your designs is out of this world and truly feels like they've come straight from a galaxy far, far away! Collaborating with you all has been an honour, and I am so grateful to be a part of this crocheting Jedi Council with such talented and inspiring individuals.

To my wonderful family, thank you for your unwavering support as I embarked on this epic adventure. To my parents, who instilled a love of Star Wars in me at a young age, you've inspired my passion for creativity and storytelling. To my husband, Nick: Without your love, encouragement, and endless patience, this book would have never happened. I love you to the Outer Rim and back. To my two little Padawans: I hope that this book shows you that no dream is too big to follow—whether it's to write your own book one day or to explore the galaxy. May the Force always guide you.

To my grandma, who brought the joy of crochet into my life: Thank you for taking me on as your apprentice and patiently teaching me the craft that has become such an important part of my journey. Love and miss you always.

A special thank you to my amazing in-laws, who generously offered countless hours of babysitting to help bring this project to life. Your support made it possible for me to focus on this dream, and I'm so grateful for you.

To all the yarn companies that generously supported this book: Your contributions brought these designs to life with the perfect textures and colours that every *Star Wars* fan will appreciate.

Finally, a huge thank you to the entire Insight Editions team. It has been an absolute pleasure to embark on this adventure with you all. Your dedication, creativity, and hard work have brought this project to life in ways I never imagined.

May the Force be with you all!

ABOUT THE AUTHOR

Leah Parker is a lifelong Star Wars fan, crochet enthusiast, and self-proclaimed crafting Jedi based in St. Albert, Alberta, Canada. Having grown up surrounded by a family who shared a love for the galaxy far, far away, Leah was inspired to combine her two passions—crocheting and Star Wars—into a project that celebrates creativity, storytelling, and fandom.

When she's not designing crochet patterns or rewatching her favourite Star Wars movies, Leah enjoys spending time with her family, sharing her love of crafting with her little Padawans, and dreaming up her next big project. She is thrilled to share this book with fellow fans and crafters, hoping it inspires others to explore their own creativity and perhaps even feel the Force as they crochet their way across the galaxy.

May the yarn be with you!

Pavilion
An imprint of HarperCollins*Publishers* Ltd
1 London Bridge Street
London SE1 9GF

www.harpercollins.co.uk

HarperCollins*Publishers*
Macken House
39/40 Mayor Street Upper,
Dublin 1
D01 C9W8
Ireland

10 9 8 7 6 5 4 3 2 1

All rights reserved. Published by Insight Editions,
San Rafael, California, in 2025.

First published in Great Britain by Pavilion
An imprint of HarperCollins*Publishers* 2025

 © & ™ 2025 LUCASFILM LTD

ISBN 978-0-00-877802-6

Publisher: Raoul Goff
SVP, Group Publisher: Vanessa Lopez
VP, Creative: Chrissy Kwasnik
VP, Manufacturing: Alix Nicholaeff
Publishing Director: Mike Degler
Editorial Director: Thom O'Hearn
Art Director: Stuart Smith
Senior Designer: Judy Wiatrek Trum
Editor: Alexis Sattler
Editorial Assistant: Gabrielle Cruz
Managing Editor: Shannon Ballesteros
Production Manager: Deena Hashem
Strategic Production Planner: Lina s Palma-Temena
Technical Editor: Julie Desjardins
Photographer: Ted Thomas
Assistant Photographer: James Newman
Prop Stylist: Elena P. Craig

Thanks to our models: Adam, Alix, Aviva, Elise, Emi, Jacqui, Jayden, Mia, Ray, and Sami
Manufactured in China by Insight Editions

10 9 8 7 6 5 4 3 2 1

All rights reserved. No part of this publication may be reproduced, stored in a retrieval system, or transmitted, in any form or by any means, electronic, mechanical, photocopying, recording or otherwise, without the prior written permission of the publishers.

Without limiting the exclusive rights of any author, contributor or the publisher of this publication, any unauthorised use of this publication to train generative artificial intelligence (AI) technologies is expressly prohibited. HarperCollins also exercise their rights under Article 4(3) of the Digital Single Market Directive 2019/790 and expressly reserve this publication from the text and data mining exception.